Everyman's Poetry

Everyman, I will go with thee,
and be thy guide

Christina Rossetti

Selected and edited by JAN MARSH

EVERYMAN

J. M. Dent · London

This book is for Diane D'Amico

Introduction and other critical apparatus
© Jan Marsh 1996

J. M. Dent
Orion Publishing Group
Orion House
5 Upper St Martin's Lane
London WC2H 9EA

Typeset by Deltatype Ltd, Ellesmere Port, Cheshire
Printed in Great Britain by
The Guernsey Press Co. Ltd, Guernsey, C.I.

British Library Cataloguing-in-Publication Data
is available upon request.

ISBN 0 460 87820 4

Contents

Note on the Author and Editor

CHRISTINA G. ROSSETTI (1830–94) was among the finest poets writing in English in the Victorian era, whose work remains popular with both general readers and scholars. It ranges from simple-seeming love lyrics and carols like 'In the bleak mid-winter' through dramatic fantasy poems like 'Goblin Market' to devotional and mystical meditations on the human and divine. Her work displays a teasing sense of humour and a Gothic imagination as well as a strong moral sense. Born into a largely Italian family in London, she was sister to two members of the Pre-Raphaelite Brotherhood, and posed for some of their early paintings. In her own right she worked at the London Penitentiary for Fallen Women, retraining young prostitutes for a respectable way of life. She published four volumes of poetry, two books for children and a collection of sparkling stories.

JAN MARSH is a biographer and critic, author of the most recent life of Christina Rossetti, published in 1994, and of the forthcoming biography of Dante Gabriel Rossetti. She studied literature at the Universities of Cambridge and Sussex, and now lectures widely on women in the Pre-Raphaelite circle and issues of gender in Victorian art and literature.

Chronology of Rossetti's Life

Year	Age	Life
1826		Marriage of Gabriele Rossetti and Frances Polidori (FLR)
1827		Birth of Maria Francesca Rossetti (MFR)
1828		Birth of Gabriel Charles Dante Rossetti (DGR)
1829		Birth of William Michael Rossetti (WMR)
1830		Birth of Christina Georgina Rossetti (CGR)
1842	11	First surviving poem 'To My Mother'
1843	12	FLR and her daughters attend Christ Church Albany Street, under Rev. William Dodsworth. Gabriele Rossetti suffers breakdown and loss of income
1844	13	MFR leaves home to become a governess
1845	14	CGR suffers nervous breakdown. WMR joins Civil Service as junior clerk. DGR at art school. MFR returns home to be language teacher
1847	16	*Verses* by Christina G. Rossetti issued by grandfather
1848	17	First commercially published poems, in *Athenaeum* (October). Engagement to James Collinson, member of PRB

Chronology of her Times

Year	Artistic Events	Historical Events
1820–1		Uprising by and suppression of Carbonari in Naples
1824	Death of Byron at Missilonghi	
1832		First Reform Act in Britain
1837		Accession of Queen Victoria
1842	Tennyson, *Poems*	
1843	Dickens, *A Christmas Carol* Carlyle, *Past and Present*	
1844	Elizabeth Barrett, *Poems*	
1845		J. H. Newman joins Church of Rome
1846–7		Famine in Ireland
1847	Charlotte Brontë, *Jane Eyre* Anne Brontë, *Agnes Grey* Emily Brontë, *Wuthering Heights* Tennyson, *The Princess*	
1848	Pre-Raphaelite Brotherhood (PRB)	Democratic revolutions in France, Germany, Austria, Poland and parts of Italy

Year	Age	Life
1850	19	Seven poems in the *Germ*. Writes *Maude: A Story for Girls*. End of engagement
1851	20	Rossetti family move to Camden Town, where CGR assists her mother with a school for young children
1852	21	CGR contributes to *The Bouquet from Marylebone Gardens*
1853	22–3	CGR resident with mother and father in Somerset
1854	23	Gabriele Rossetti dies in London. CGR meets Mary Howitt, author and editor, and has poems published in anthologies. Aunt Eliza Polidori joins Florence Nightingale's nursing team
1856	25	*The Lost Titian* published in *The Crayon* (New York)
1857	26	*Nick* published in the *National Magazine*
1859	28	CGR joins staff of Diocesan Penitentiary for Fallen Women at Highgate. Writes 'Goblin Market'. 'In the Round Tower at Jhansi' and 'Maude Clare' published in *Once a Week*
1860	29	MFR begins attachment to All Saints Sisterhood, Marylebone. DGR marries Elizabeth Siddal
1861	30	'Up-Hill' published in *Macmillan's Magazine* (February); CGR prepares her first collection
1862	31	Death of Elizabeth Siddal Rossetti. *Goblin Market and Other Poems* published (April). CGR visits France
1862–4	31–3	Meets fellow poets Jean Ingelow and Dora Greenwell. Joins Portfolio Society, informal writers' and artists' group founded by Barbara Bodichon

Year	Artistic Events	Historical Events
1850	Death of Wordsworth Tennyson, *In Memoriam*	Roman Catholic hierarchy established in Britain
1851		Napoleon III assumes power in France The Great Exhibition
1852	Harriet Beecher Stowe, *Uncle Tom's Cabin* (British edition)	
1853	Elizabeth Gaskell, *Ruth*	
1854	Tennyson, *The Charge of the Light Brigade*	Crimean War declared by Britain and France against Russia; Florence Nightingale leads nursing team to Scutari; Gold Rush in Australia
1856	William Morris and Edward Burne-Jones, *Oxford & Cambridge Magazine*	Feminist campaign for Married Women's Property Act
1857	Elizabeth Barrett Browning, *Aurora Leigh* Baudelaire, *Les Fleurs du Mal*	Indian Mutiny
1859	Charles Darwin, *The Origin of Species* Mill, *On Liberty* Tennyson, *Idylls of the King*	
1860	Ruskin, *Unto this Last*	Liberation and eventual unification of Italy
1861	Death of Elizabeth Barrett Browning	American Civil War begins Death of Prince Albert
1862		Emancipation Proclamation by President Lincoln Formation of Morris & Co

Year	Age	Life
1865	35	Travels to Switzerland and northern Italy with FLR and WMR
1866	36	*Poems* published by Roberts Bros, Boston. *The Prince's Progress and Other Poems* published by Macmillan. CGR declines proposal from Charles Cayley
1867	37	Three religious stories in the *Churchman's Shilling Magazine*. Rossetti family moves to Euston Square, Bloomsbury
1870	40	Publication of *Poems* by DGR. Publication of *Commonplace and Other Short Stories*
1870–2	40–2	CGR suffers serious illness (Graves' disease)
1872	42	Publication of *Sing-Song* by Dalziels for Routledge, with illustrations by Arthur Hughes. DGR suffers nervous collapse and suicidal paranoia
1873	43	WMR becomes engaged to Lucy Madox Brown. MFR begins novitiate at All Saints' Sisterhood
1874	44	Publication of *Annus Domini: A Prayer for Each Day of the Year* and *Speaking Likenesses*
1875	45	Collected edition of *Poems* published by Macmillan
1876	46	CGR, FLR and aunts move to Torrington Square, Bloomsbury. Death of MFR
1878–80	48–50	CGR attends lectures on *Divine Comedy* and corresponds with Augusta Webster on women's franchise

Year	Artistic Events	Historical Events
1865	Carroll, *Alice in Wonderland*	American Civil War ends Foundation of Vassar College, USA
1866	Swinburne, *Poems and Ballads*	
1867		Second British Reform Act Women's suffrage societies launched in Britain and USA
1868	William Morris, *The Earthly Paradise* Robert Browning, *The Ring and the Book* Mill, *The Subjection of Women*	Gladstone, PM
1869	Arnold, *Culture and Anarchy*	Foundation of Girton College; Suez Canal opened
1870	Death of Dickens	Franco-Prussian War; Elementary Education Act
1871		Paris Commune
1872	George Eliot, *Middlemarch*	
1873	Pater, *Studies in the History of the Renaissance*	
1874		Annexation of Gold Coast (Ghana) by Britain
1876	Ibsen, *A Doll's House* Alice Meynell, *Preludes*	Queen Victoria proclaimed Empress of India; university entrance and medical education opened to British women

Year	Age	Life
1879	49	Publication of *Seek and Find: Short Studies of the Benedicite* by SPCK
1880	50	CGR involved in anti-vivisection campaign
1881	51	Publication of *A Pageant and Other Poems* and *Called to be Saints: the Minor Festivals devotionally studied*
1882	52	Death of DGR. Publication of *Poems, New Series* by Roberts Bros, Boston
1883	53	Publication of *Letter and Spirit: Notes on the Commandments* by SPCK. Death of Charles Cayley. CGR involved in child protection campaign
1885	55	Publication of *Time Flies, A Reading Diary* by SPCK. Start of friendships with Katharine Tynan and Lisa Wilson
1886	56	Death of FLR
1890	60	Publication of enlarged edition of *Poems* by Macmillan
1892	62	Publication of *The Face of the Deep: a commentary on the Apocalypse* by SPCK. Surgery for cancer
1893	63	Publication of *Verses* by SPCK
1894	63–4	CGR dies (29 December)

Year	Artistic Events	Historical Events
1881	James, *Portrait of a Lady* Wilde, *Poems*	Married Women's Property Act
1882		British occupation of Egypt
1883	Olive Schreiner, *Story of an African Farm*	
1885	W. T. Stead, *The Maiden Tribute of Modern Babylon*	Age of sexual consent raised to 16; British war against Sudan Death of Gen. Gordon at Khartoum; foundation of Socialist League
1886		Irish Home Rule Bill defeated
1889	Death of Browning Yeats, *Wanderings of Oisin*	
1890	Death of Tennyson and Newman Morris, *News from Nowhere* Emily Dickinson, *Poems*	
1894		Woman Suffrage Act in New Zealand

Introduction

This selection from Christina Rossetti's poetry displays the range of her work, from short lyrics and dramatic ballads to longer narratives, monologues, elaborate sonnets and religious meditations. It includes some of her poems for children and her adult fantasy *Goblin Market*.

Though Victorian, her poems speak directly to us today in a lively and often colloquial voice that sounds open and personal but is often teasing or reticent, and always suggests more than is said. Above all, Christina Rossetti's writing is vivid, musical, imaginative.

It is therefore enjoyable and easy to understand, though not as simple as it first appears. Very often the poems have double, deeper meanings, or hint at a mysterious, unrevealed subject that seems to lie just beneath as well as on the polished surface. One reason for this is that at its finest poetry is not simply transposable into prose, but actually exists in its own verbal dimension where sound and sense, image and meaning are fused – the crucible of that synthetic and magical power, in Coleridge's words, that we call poetic imagination and that is the source of textual pleasure.

Another reason is that Christina Rossetti, as a Victorian citizen and Christian believer, looked on everything connected with the material world (including words and images) as imperfect intimations or symbols of the spiritual world – 'heaven' in her cosmology – which could not be fully comprehended. But we do not need to share her beliefs to admire her poems, which with those of Milton, Herbert, Donne, Blake, Hopkins and Eliot, share in and contribute to the long English tradition of religious imagery drawn from the Judaeo-Christian legacy.

Christina Rossetti was born in London on 5 December 1830, and died on 29 December 1894, aged sixty-four. Queen Victoria came to the throne in 1837 and died in 1901, so Christina Rossetti's life spanned nearly the whole of the period now known as the Victorian age – the age of railways, industrial development, political democracy, urban expansion, global exploration, the British

Empire. It was also an age of education, rising prosperity, widening access to art, literature, illustrated magazines and popular entertainment.

As her surname indicates, Christina's family was of Italian origin. Her father, Professor Gabriele Rossetti, was a political refugee from Naples, one of the many exiled for their participation in the struggle for Italian freedom and unity. He was also a poet and scholar, whose main research was into the work of Dante Alighieri, author of the *Divine Comedy*. Christina's mother, Frances Polidori, was a teacher before marriage and herself the daughter of an Italian father and English mother; Frances's brother, John Polidori, who died before Christina was born, was briefly famous as Byron's physician and author of *The Vampyre*.

The Rossetti family was bi-lingual, though speaking mainly English. Christina was the youngest of four. Her elder sister Maria became a teacher and eventually an Anglican nun. Her two brothers were Dante Gabriel, who became a famous painter and poet, and William Michael, who was both a civil servant and an art critic; together they were founder-members of the Pre-Raphaelite Brotherhood, or PRB, in 1848. Christina and Maria were educated at home by their mother. From around 1840 the family was short of money, owing to Professor Rossetti's ill health. At the age of fourteen Christina herself suffered a severe breakdown, and at the same time came under the influence of the Anglo-Catholic or Tractarian movement in the Church of England, which inspired lifelong devotion in both sisters.

In 1847 her paternal grandfather printed a small collection of her poems – forty-six in all – on his own press. The following year she had two poems accepted by the *Athenaeum*, a leading liberal and literary weekly. At the same time she was drawn into the excitement surrounding the PRB group of avant-garde painters, whose innovative works startled the contemporary art world. Christina was the model for the young Virgin Mary in two of D. G. Rossetti's best known paintings, but she did not otherwise pose for the Pre-Raphaelite painters, as is sometimes claimed. Several of her poems were published in the PRB magazine, the short-lived *Germ*, in 1850.

From the outset, humour and sharp observation co-existed alongside pathos and music in her poetry. Overall, the mournful mode may dominate, but the sprightly, satirical voice is equally characteristic, and her sensibility is seldom sentimental. Taking refuge partly in invalidism, she sought no full-time career outside literature, but in 1854 she applied unsuccessfully to join Florence Nightingale's nursing team in the Crimea and for some years assisted her mother running a small private school. From 1859 to 1864 she was a voluntary residential worker at the Highgate Penitentiary for Fallen Women, helping to reclaim and re-train young prostitutes. In her writings she expresses ambivalence towards the position of women as prescribed by Victorian patriarchy, being partly and publicly submissive to religious teachings on the subject, but partly rebellious and subversive. She was on friendly terms with several leading feminists in the 1850s and 60s, but later expressed her opposition to women's suffrage. Her political energies, in an age when women did not have the right to vote, were directed in defence of the weak and vulnerable, against the sexual exploitation of girls and in anti-vivisection campaigns for animal rights.

Her emotional life was one of disappointment. At the age of eighteen she was engaged to James Collinson, a member of the PRB, who two years later withdrew from both the Brotherhood and the engagement after re-joining the Catholic Church to forsake other commitment for a life of religious service. Christina's immature heart was badly broken and took years to heal. In the early 1860s she conceived an affection for Charles Cayley, a shy, unworldly scholar and translator, but when he finally proposed marriage, she declined on the grounds of religious (and one may suspect also personal) incompatibility, although remaining his good friend and literary executor. Her fine sonnet sequence *Monna Innominata*, written around 1880, is put into the voice of an unknown (*innominata*) poetess, unhappy in love, speaking to the lover she is prevented from joining by a barrier 'held sacred by both, yet not such as to render mutual love incompatible with mutual honour'.

At an early age, however, she protested against her poems being read as 'love personals' describing her own experiences. She was in fact too reticent to write in a confessional mode, and the speaking voice in many of her poems is a mask, or persona, expressing and dramatising a range of emotion which cannot simply be read back into the poet's own life.

After initial early success, Rossetti found it hard to get her poems accepted for publication, until in 1862 Macmillan brought out her first collection, *Goblin Market and Other Poems*. As her brother

William, who later edited her work, commented: by this date she thought that recognition – the bay wreath of fame – had been too long delayed. Though 'the most modest of poets', she did not undervalue the quality of her work. She was, according to the poet Swinburne, 'the Jael who led our hosts to victory' in terms of new energy and imagery in poetry. But while *Goblin Market* was hailed as the work of a remarkable and original poet, her later volumes *The Prince's Progress and Other Poems* (1866) and *A Pageant and Other Poems* (1881) added to her reputation – which was always higher in America than Britain – without extending it. She also published a collection of short stories in 1870, a book of original nursery rhymes called *Sing-Song* in 1872 and a volume of children's stories in 1874, together with five books of religious and devotional meditation. Of the devotional works, *Time Flies* (1885) is the most interesting, both because it is most personal and because it mixes poetry and prose.

Guided by strong moral disapproval of boastfulness or 'conceit', Christina Rossetti did not seek fame or indulge in self-promotion. Socially she was retiring, though with an acerbic wit and sharp judgements, especially on religious matters. She encouraged the work of younger writers where she could do so wholeheartedly, with firm opinions on what constituted true poetry as opposed to mere versification. She valued her own work highly but not excessively, often lamenting that 'the muse' had deserted her.

The Rossetti family was repeatedly struck by tragedy. After a brief marriage, her brother Gabriel's wife Elizabeth Siddal died of an opium overdose in 1862, and ten years later Gabriel himself succumbed to paranoid delusions of persecution and to mental breakdown; after a long decline he died in 1882. Maria Rossetti died of cancer in 1876, aged forty-nine, a loss Christina found hard to bear. Thereafter she nursed her mother and two aged aunts through to their deaths. William married in 1874, but as his wife's health deteriorated she turned against him, causing much distress. Christina herself contracted breast cancer, dying at the end of 1894 after a painful operation and months of suffering. William survived until 1919, editing both his sister's and brother's poetry and correspondence for publication.

At her death she left a large number of unpublished poems, mainly written in the first half of her life. In later years she wrote more sparingly, or did not preserve work unworthy of publication.

Few rough drafts survive; generally speaking the texts are taken from final copy manuscripts. On occasion poems were pruned before publication, and in the early years her brother Gabriel gave useful advice on the selection and titling of poems. Rossetti seldom wrote with a title in mind. Sometimes she added a loose or misleading title once the poem was complete. Fairly often, short poems were left untitled, or called simply 'Song'.

Perhaps the most attractive is 'Winter: My Secret', one of the last poems in this compact collection of one hundred pieces. As Professor Isobel Armstrong writes, this is a piece 'in which the wit and lyric energy of Rossetti's work come together. It is a poem about secrecy and reserve, prohibition, taboo, revealing and concealing, and is almost a summa of her work. Provocative and flirtatious and yet deeply reticent.'

The literary influences on Christina Rossetti's work are wide and varied, ranging from Edmund Spenser and Thomas à Kempis to Alexander Pope and George Crabbe, from John Keats to Elizabeth Barrett Browning and Edgar Allan Poe. Her imagination was shaped by Gothic tales and the *Song of Songs*, by Italian opera, Dante's *Inferno*, Border Ballads, Petrarch's sonnets. She wrote silly poems about pigs and profound poems about frogs. She wrote about dreams, nightmares, Romantic death. Her work is infused with erotic desire and with ascetic denial. As critic Anthony Harrison writes: 'her concerns (and her poetry) are at once traditional and radically innovative, sincere and artificial, self-effacing and self-promoting, self-expressive and parodic'.

In her own terms, she 'preferred to take what came when it came', and professed to having no system or purposeful scheme in poetry. This has been taken to mean her verses bubbled up spontaneously, without effort. In fact, she was careful and thoughtful in composition, aiming only to leave no trace of the process involved, so that even long works like *Goblin Market*, her masterpiece, seem as if completed in a single impulse. Not everything was successful: of over a thousand poems in total, some are weak or repetitive. But, as Isobel Armstrong has recently commented, in the depth and range and in the beauty and boldness of her language, Christina Rossetti may be ranked with Tennyson and Browning among the best poets of the Victorian age. On Tennyson's death in 1892, indeed, many contemporaries regarded her as the finest living poet in Britain. 'If only the Queen would consult me as to whom to make Poet Laureate!' declared Lewis Carroll. 'I would say, "For once, Madam, take a lady!" '

Christina Rossetti's reputation declined dramatically in the twentieth century, owing partly to its religious cast and partly to the advent of Modernism. Her modest self-abnegation in lines like 'Give me the lowest place' also tended to diminish her stature in the shadow of Yeats, Eliot, Pound and Auden. Even her gender was held against her by critics and scholars, who criticised her limited range and 'weak' intellect, with the result that although her words such as 'In the bleak mid-winter' and 'Remember me when I am gone away' were sung and quoted by millions, her work as a whole was ignored. It has always been admired by poets, however, for its metrical brilliance and verbal bravery. And as Victorian poetry returned to critical favour from the 1980s onwards, and as feminist perspectives entered the mainstream, so Christina Rossetti has slowly regained her rightful place in the literary canon.

To a large extent, critical neglect has been beneficial, since it obliges readers to form their own responses to her work rather than relying on received opinion. Fortunately, the poems themselves encourage this, springing off the page with irresistible grace and spirit. Even where the thought is complex, there is no difficulty or obscurity for its own sake. All is carefully crafted. 'Perhaps the nearest approach to a "method" I can lay claim to was a distinct aim at conciseness,' she once wrote to an enquirer; 'after a while I received a hint from my sister that my love of conciseness tended to make my writing obscure and I then endeavoured to avoid obscurity as well as diffuseness'. She was also helped by reading everything she wrote, both prose and verse, aloud to her sister and mother.

Reading aloud is still the best approach to Christina Rossetti's poetry, which is above all an aural as well as intellectual experience. Some archaic words and phrases have to be negotiated, but seldom detract from the simple and subtle pleasures of speaking and listening to her lines. Try it and see.

JAN MARSH

Christina Rossetti

Advent

Earth grown old, yet still so green,
      Deep beneath her crust of cold
Nurses fire unfelt, unseen:
      Earth grown old.

      We who live are quickly told:
Millions more lie hid between
      Inner swathings of her fold.

When will fire break up her screen?
      When will life burst through her mould?
Earth, earth, earth, thy cold is keen,
      Earth grown old.

All Heaven is Blazing

All heaven is blazing yet
   With the meridian sun:
Make haste, unshadowing sun, make haste to set;
   O lifeless life, have done.
I choose what once I chose;
   What once I willed, I will:
Only the heart its own bereavement knows;
   O clamorous heart, lie still.

That which I chose, I choose;
   That which I willed, I will;
That which I once refused, I still refuse:
   O hope deferred, be still.
That which I chose, and choose
   And will is Jesus' will:

He hath not lost his life who seems to lose:
O hope deferred, hope still.

An Apple Gathering

I plucked pink blossoms from mine apple-tree
  And wore them all that evening in my hair:
Then in due season when I went to see
  I found no apples there.

With dangling basket all along the grass
  As I had come I went the self-same track:
My neighbours mocked me while they saw me pass
  So empty-handed back.

Lilian and Lilias smiled in trudging by,
  Their heaped-up basket teazed me like a jeer;
Sweet-voiced they sang beneath the sunset sky,
  Their mother's home was near.

Plump Gertrude passed me with her basket full,
  A stronger hand than hers helped it along;
A voice talked with her through the shadows cool
  More sweet to me than song.

Ah Willie, Willie, was my love less worth
  Than apples with their green leaves piled above?
I counted rosiest apples on the earth
  Of far less worth than love.

So once it was with me you stooped to talk
  Laughing and listening in this very lane;
To think that by this way we used to walk
  We shall not walk again!

I let my neighbours pass me, ones and twos
   And groups; the latest said the night grew chill,
And hastened: but I loitered; while the dews
   Fell fast I loitered still.

At Home

When I was dead, my spirit turned
   To seek the much-frequented house.
I passed the door, and saw my friends
   Feasting beneath green orange-boughs;
From hand to hand they pushed the wine,
   They sucked the pulp of plum and peach;
They sang, they jested, and they laughed,
   For each was loved of each.

I listened to their honest chat.
   Said one; 'Tomorrow we shall be
Plod plod along the featureless sands,
   And coasting miles and miles of sea.'
Said one: 'Before the turn of tide
   We will achieve the eyrie-seat.'
Said one: 'Tomorrow shall be like
   Today, but much more sweet.'

'Tomorrow,' said they, strong with hope,
   And dwelt upon the pleasant way:
'Tomorrow,' cried they one and all,
   While no one spoke of yesterday.
Their life stood full at blessed noon;
   I, only I, had passed away:
'Tomorrow and today,' they cried;
   I was of yesterday.

I shivered comfortless, but cast
   No chill across the tablecloth;
I all-forgotten shivered, sad

To stay and yet to part how loth:
I passed from the familiar room,
   I who from love had passed away,
Like the remembrance of a guest
   That tarrieth but a day.

from Sing-Song

Baby lies so fast asleep
   That we cannot wake her:
Will the Angels clad in white
   Fly from heaven to take her?

Baby lies so fast asleep
   That no pain can grieve her;
Put a snowdrop in her hand,
   Kiss her once and leave her.

'Behold, I stand at the door and knock'

Who standeth at the gate? – A woman old,
   A widow from the husband of her love:
'O Lady, stay; this wind is piercing cold,
   Oh look at the keen frosty moon above;
I have no home, am hungry, feeble, poor:'—
   'I'm really very sorry, but I can
   Do nothing for you, there's the clergyman,'—
The Lady said, and shivering closed the door.

Who standeth at the gate? – Way-worn and pale,
   A grey-haired man asks charity again:
'Kind Lady, I have journeyed far, and fail

Thro' weariness; for I have begged in vain
Some shelter, and can find no lodging-place:'—
    She answered: 'There's the Workhouse very near,
    Go, for they'll certainly receive you there:'—
Then shut the door against his pleading face.

Who standeth at the gate? – A stunted child,
    Her sunk eyes sharpened with precocious care:
'O Lady, save me from a home defiled,
    From shameful sights and sounds that taint the air.
Take pity on me, teach me something good;'—
    'For shame, why don't you work instead of cry?—
    I keep no young impostors here, not I;'—
She slammed the door, indignant where she stood.

Who standeth at the gate, and will be heard?—
    Arise, O woman, from thy comforts now:
Go forth again to speak the careless word,
    The cruel word unjust, with hardened brow.
But Who is This, That standeth not to pray
    As once, but terrible to judge thy sin?
    This, Whom thou wouldst not succour, nor take in,
Nor teach, but leave to perish by the way?—

'Thou didst it not unto the least of these,
    And in them hast not done it unto Me.
Thou wast as a princess, rich and at ease,
    Now sit in dust and howl for poverty.
Three times I stood beseeching at thy gate,
    Three times I came to bless thy soul and save:
    But now I come to judge for what I gave,
And now at length thy sorrow is too late.'

A Better Resurrection

I have no wit, no words, no tears;
  My heart within me like a stone
Is numbed too much for hopes or fears.
  Look right, look left, I dwell alone;
I lift mine eyes, but dimmed with grief
  No everlasting hills I see;
My life is in the falling leaf:
    O Jesus, quicken me.

My life is like a faded leaf,
  My harvest dwindled to a husk:
Truly my life is void and brief
  And tedious in the barren dusk;
My life is like a frozen thing,
  No bud nor greenness can I see;
Yet rise it shall – the sap of Spring;
    O Jesus, rise in me.

My life is like a broken bowl,
  A broken bowl that cannot hold
One drop of water for my soul
  Or cordial in the searching cold.
Cast in the fire the perished thing;
  Melt and remould it, till it be
A royal cup for Him, my King:
    O Jesus, drink of me.

Bird or Beast?

Did any bird come flying
  After Adam and Eve,
When the door was shut against them
  And they sat down to grieve?

I think not Eve's peacock
    Splendid to see,
And I think not Adam's eagle;
    But a dove may be.

Did any beast come pushing
    Through the thorny hedge
Into the thorny thistly world,
    Out from Eden's edge?

I think not a lion,
    Though his strength is such;
But an innocent loving lamb
    May have done as much.

If the dove preached from her bough,
    And the lamb from his sod,
The lamb and the dove
    Were preachers sent from God.

A Birthday

My heart is like a singing bird
    Whose nest is in a watered shoot;
My heart is like an apple-tree
    Whose boughs are bent with thickset fruit;
My heart is like a rainbow shell
    That paddles in a halcyon sea;
My heart is gladder than all these
    Because my love is come to me.

Raise me a dais of silk and down;
    Hang it with vair and purple dyes;
Carve it in doves and pomegranates,
    And peacocks with a hundred eyes;
Work it in gold and silver grapes,

In leaves and silver fleurs-de-lys;
Because the birthday of my life
   Is come, my love is come to me.

A Christmas Carol

In the bleak mid-winter
   Frosty wind made moan,
Earth stood hard as iron,
   Water like a stone;
Snow had fallen, snow on snow,
   Snow on snow,
In the bleak mid-winter
   Long ago.

Our God, Heaven cannot hold Him
   Nor earth sustain;
Heaven and earth shall flee away
   When He comes to reign;
In the bleak mid-winter
   A stable-place sufficed
The Lord God Almighty
   Jesus Christ.

Enough for Him, whom cherubim
   Worship night and day,
A breastful of milk
   And a mangerful of hay;
Enough for Him, whom angels
   Fall down before,
The ox and ass and camel
   Which adore.

Angels and archangels
   May have gathered there,
Cherubim and seraphim

Thronged the air;
But only His mother
    In her maiden bliss
Worshipped the Beloved
    With a kiss.

What can I give Him,
    Poor as I am?
If I were a shepherd
    I would bring a lamb,
If I were a Wise Man
    I would do my part,—
Yet what I can I give Him,
    Give my heart.

A Coast: Nightmare

I have a love in ghostland—
    Early found, ah me, how early lost!—
Blood-red seaweeds drip along that coastland
    By the strong sea wrenched and tossed.
In every creek there slopes a dead man's islet,
    And such an one in every bay;
All unripened in the unended twilight:
    For there comes neither night nor day.

Unripe harvest there hath none to reap it
    From the watery misty place;
Unripe vineyard there hath none to keep it
    In unprofitable space.
Living flocks and herds are nowhere found there;
    Only ghosts in flocks and shoals:
Indistinguished hazy ghosts surround there
    Meteors whirling on their poles;
Indistinguished hazy ghosts abound there;

Troops, yea swarms, of dead men's souls.—

Have they towns to live in?—
　　They have towers and towns from sea to sea;
Of each town the gates are seven;
　　Of one of these each ghost is free.
Civilians, soldiers, seamen,
　　Of one town each ghost is free:
They are ghastly men those ghostly freemen:
　　Such a sight may you not see.—

How know you that your lover
　　Of death's tideless waters stoops to drink?—
Me by night doth mouldy darkness cover,
　　It makes me quake to think:
All night long I feel his presence hover
　　Through the darkness black as ink.

Without a voice he tells me
　　The wordless secrets of death's deep:
If I sleep, he like a trump compels me
　　To stalk forth in my sleep:
If I wake, he rides me like a nightmare;
　　I feel my hair stand up, my body creep:
Without light I see a blasting sight there,
　　See a secret I must keep.

Cobwebs

It is a land with neither night nor day,
　　Nor heat nor cold, nor any wind, nor rain,
　　Nor hills nor valleys: but one even plain
Stretches through long unbroken miles away,
While through the sluggish air a twilight grey
　　Broodeth: no moons or seasons wax and wane,
　　No ebb and flow are there along the main,

No bud-time, no leaf-falling there for aye:–
No ripple on the sea, no shifting sand,
   No beat of wings to stir the stagnant space:
No pulse of life through all the loveless land
And loveless sea; no trace of days before,
   No guarded home, no toil-won resting-place
No future hope, no fear for evermore.

Confluents

As rivers seek the sea,
   Much more deep than they,
So my soul seeks thee
   Far away:
As running rivers moan
On their course alone,
   So I moan
   Left alone.

As the delicate rose
   To the sun's sweet strength
Doth herself unclose,
   Breadth and length;
So spreads my heart to thee
Unveiled utterly,
   I to thee
   Utterly.

As morning dew exhales
   Sunwards pure and free
So my spirit fails
   After thee:
As dew leaves not a trace
On the green earth's face;
   I, no trace
   On thy face.

Its goal the river knows,
    Dewdrops find a way,
Sunlight cheers the rose
    In her day:
Shall I, lone sorrow past,
Find thee at the last?
    Sorrow past,
    Thee at last?

The Convent Threshold

There's blood between us, love, my love,
There's father's blood, there's brother's blood;
And blood's a bar I cannot pass:
I choose the stairs that mount above,
Stair after golden sky-ward stair,
To city and to sea of glass.
My lily feet are soiled with mud,
With scarlet mud which tells a tale
Of hope that was, of guilt that was,
Of love that shall not yet avail;
Alas, my heart, if I could bare
My heart, this selfsame stain is there:
I seek the sea of glass and fire
To wash the spot, to burn the snare;
Lo, stairs are meant to lift us higher:
Mount with me, mount the kindled stair.

Your eyes look earthward, mine look up.
I see the far-off city grand,
Beyond the hills a watered land,
Beyond the gulf a gleaming strand
Of mansions where the righteous sup;
Who sleep at ease among their trees,
Or wake to sing a cadenced hymn
With Cherubim and Seraphim.

They bore the cross, they drained the cup,
Racked, roasted, crushed, wrenched limb from limb,
They the offscouring of the world:
The heaven of starry heavens unfurled,
The sun before their face is dim.

You looking earthward, what see you?
Milk-white, wine-flushed among the vines,
Up and down leaping, to and fro,
Most glad, most full, made strong with wines,
Blooming as peaches pearled with dew,
Their golden windy hair afloat,
Love-music warbling in their throat,
Young men and women come and go.

You linger, yet the time is short:
Flee for your life, gird up your strength
To flee; the shadows stretched at length
Show that day wanes, that night draws nigh;
Flee to the mountain, tarry not.
Is this a time for smile and sigh,
For songs among the secret trees
Where sudden blue birds nest and sport?
The time is short and yet you stay:
Today, while it is called today,
Kneel, wrestle, knock, do violence, pray;
Today is short, tomorrow nigh:
Why will you die? why will you die?

You sinned with me a pleasant sin:
Repent with me, for I repent.
Woe's me the lore I must unlearn!
Woe's me that easy way we went,
So rugged when I would return!
How long until my sleep begin,
How long shall stretch these nights and days?
Surely, clean Angels cry, she prays;
She laves her soul with tedious tears:
How long must stretch these years and years?

I turn from you my cheeks and eyes,
My hair which you shall see no more—
Alas for joy that went before,
For joy that dies, for love that dies!
Only my lips still turn to you,
My livid lips that cry, Repent!
O weary life, O weary Lent,
O weary time whose stars are few!

How should I rest in Paradise,
Or sit on steps of heaven alone?
If Saints and Angels spoke of love,
Should I not answer from my throne:
Have pity upon me, ye my friends,
For I have heard the sound thereof.
Should I not turn with yearning eyes,
Turn earthwards with a pitiful pang?
Oh save me from a pang in heaven!
By all the gifts we took and gave,
Repent, repent, and be forgiven.
This life is long, but yet it ends;
Repent and purge your soul and save:
No gladder song the morning stars
Upon their birthday morning sang
Than Angels sing when one repents.

I tell you what I dreamed last night.
A spirit with transfigured face
Fire-footed clomb an infinite space.
I heard his hundred pinions clang,
Heaven-bells rejoicing rang and rang,
Heaven-air was thrilled with subtle scents,
Worlds spun upon their rushing cars:
He mounted shrieking 'Give me light!'
Still light was poured on him, more light;
Angels, Archangels he outstripped,
Exultant in exceeding might,
And trod the skirts of Cherubim.
Still 'Give me light,' he shrieked; and dipped
His thirsty face, and drank a sea,

Athirst with thirst it could not slake.
I saw him, drunk with knowledge, take
From aching brows the aureole crown—
His locks writhed like a cloven snake—
He left his throne to grovel down
And lick the dust of Seraphs' feet:
For what is knowledge duly weighed?
Knowledge is strong, but love is sweet;
Yea all the progress he had made
Was but to learn that all is small
Save love, for love is all in all.

I tell you what I dreamed last night:
It was not dark, it was not light,
Cold dews had drenched my plenteous hair
Through clay; you came to seek me there,
And 'Do you dream of me?' you said.
My heart was dust that used to leap
To you; I answered half asleep:
'My pillow is damp, my sheets are red,
There's a leaden tester to my bed:
Find you a warmer playfellow,
A warmer pillow for your head,
A kinder love to love than mine.'
You wrung your hands: while I, like lead,
Crushed downwards through the sodden earth:
You smote your hands but not in mirth,
And reeled but were not drunk with wine.

For all night long I dreamed of you:
I woke and prayed against my will,
Then slept to dream of you again.
At length I rose and knelt and prayed:
I cannot write the words I said,
My words were slow, my tears were few;
But through the dark my silence spoke
Like thunder. When this morning broke,
My face was pinched, my hair was grey,
And frozen blood was on the sill
Where stifling in my struggle I lay.

If now you saw me you would say:
Where is the face I used to love?
And I would answer: Gone before;
It tarries veiled in Paradise.
When once the morning star shall rise,
When earth with shadow flees away
And we stand safe within the door,
Then you shall lift the veil thereof.
Look up, rise up: for far above
Our palms are grown, our place is set;
There we shall meet as once we met,
And love with old familiar love.

Cousin Kate

I was a cottage maiden
   Hardened by sun and air,
Contented with my cottage mates,
   Not mindful I was fair.
Why did a great lord find me out,
   And praise my flaxen hair?
Why did a great lord find me out
   To fill my heart with care?

He lured me to his palace home—
   Woe's me for joy thereof—
To lead a shameless shameful life,
   His plaything and his love.
He wore me like a silken knot,
   He changed me like a glove;
So now I moan, an unclean thing,
   Who might have been a dove.

O Lady Kate, my cousin Kate,
   You grew more fair than I:
He saw you at your father's gate,

Chose you, and cast me by.
He watched your steps along the lane,
    Your work among the rye;
He lifted you from mean estate
    To sit with him on high.

Because you were so good and pure
    He bound you with his ring:
The neighbours call you good and pure,
    Call me an outcast thing.
Even so I sit and howl in dust,
    You sit in gold and sing:
Now which of us has tenderer heart?
    You had the stronger wing.

O cousin Kate, my love was true,
    Your love was writ in sand:
If he had fooled not me but you,
    If you stood where I stand,
He'd not have won me with his love
    Nor bought me with his land;
I would have spit into his face
    And not have taken his hand.

Yet I've a gift you have not got,
    And seem not like to get:
For all your clothes and wedding-ring
    I've little doubt you fret.
My fair-haired son, my shame, my pride,
    Cling closer, closer yet:
Your father would give lands for one
    To wear his coronet.

Day-Dreams

Gazing through her chamber window
    Sits my soul's dear soul:
Looking northward, looking southward,
    Looking to the goal,
Looking back without control.

I have strewn thy path, beloved,
    With plumed meadowsweet,
Iris and pale perfumed lilies,
    Roses most complete:
Wherefore pause on listless feet?

But she sits and never answers,
    Gazing, gazing still
On swift fountain, shadowed valley,
    Cedared sunlit hill:
Who can guess or read her will?

Who can guess or read the spirit
    Shrined within her eyes,
Part a longing, part a languor,
    Part a mere surprise,
While slow mists do rise and rise?

Is it love she looks and longs for,
    Is it rest or peace,
Is it slumber self-forgetful
    In its utter ease,
Is it one or all of these?

So she sits and doth not answer
    With her dreaming eyes,
With her languid look delicious
    Almost paradise,
Less than happy, over-wise.

Answer me, O self-forgetful—

Or of what beside?—
Is it day-dream of a maiden,
   Vision of a bride,
Is it knowledge, love, or pride?

Cold she sits through all my kindling,
   Deaf to all I pray:
I have wasted might and wisdom,
   Wasted night and day:
Deaf she dreams to all I say.

Now if I could guess her secret,
   Were it worth the guess?—
Time is lessening, hope is lessening,
   Love grows less and less:
What care I for no or yes?

I will give her stately burial,
   Though, when she lies dead:
For dear memory of the past time,
   Of her royal head,
Of the much I strove and said.

I will give her stately burial,
   Stately willow-branches bent:
Have her carved in alabaster,
   As she dreamed and leant
While I wondered what she meant.

Despised and Rejected

My sun has set, I dwell
In darkness as a dead man out of sight;
And none remains, not one, that I should tell
To him mine evil plight
This bitter night.

I will make fast my door
That hollow friends may trouble me no more.

'Friend, open to Me.' – Who is this that calls?
Nay, I am deaf as are my walls:
Cease crying, for I will not hear
Thy cry of hope or fear.
Others were dear,
Others forsook me: what art thou indeed
That I should heed
Thy lamentable need?
Hungry should feed,
Or stranger lodge thee here?

'Friend, My Feet bleed.
Open thy door to Me and comfort Me.'
I will not open, trouble me no more.
Go on thy way footsore,
I will not rise and open unto thee.

'Then is it nothing to thee? Open, see
Who stands to plead with thee.
Open, lest I should pass thee by, and thou
One day entreat My Face
And howl for grace,
And I be deaf as thou art now.
Open to Me.'

Then I cried out upon him: Cease,
Leave me in peace:
Fear not that I should crave
Aught thou mayst have.
Leave me in peace, yea trouble me no more,
Lest I arise and chase thee from my door.
What, shall I not be let
Alone, that thou dost vex me yet?

But all night long that voice spake urgently:
'Open to Me.'
Still harping in mine ears:

'Rise, let Me in.'
Pleading with tears:
'Open to Me that I may come to thee.'
While the dew dropped, while the dark hours were cold:
'My Feet bleed, see My Face,
See My Hands bleed that bring thee grace,
My Heart doth bleed for thee,
Open to Me.'

So till the break of day:
Then died away
That voice, in silence as of sorrow;
Then footsteps echoing like a sigh
Passed me by,
Lingering footsteps slow to pass.
On the morrow
I saw upon the grass
Each footprint marked in blood, and on my door
The mark of blood for evermore.

from Sonnets of Later Life

A dream there is wherein we are fain to scream,
    While struggling with ourselves we cannot speak:
    And much of all our waking life, as weak
And misconceived, eludes us like the dream.
For half life's seemings are not what they seem,
    And vain the laughs we laugh, the shrieks we shriek;
    Yea, all is vain that mars the settled meek
Contented quiet of our daily theme.
When I was young I deemed that sweets are sweet:
    But now I deem some searching bitters are
    Sweeter than sweets, and more refreshing far,
        And to be relished more, and more desired,
And more to be pursued on eager feet,
        On feet untired, and still on feet though tired.

A Dumb Friend

I planted a young tree when I was young:
But now the tree is grown and I am old:
There wintry robin shelters from the cold
    And tunes his silver tongue.

A green and living tree I planted it,
A glossy-foliaged tree of evergreen:
All through the noontide heat it spread a screen
    Whereunder I might sit.

But now I only watch it where it towers:
I, sitting at my window, watch it tossed
By rattling gale or silvered by the frost;
    Or, when sweet summer flowers,

Wagging its round green head with stately grace
In tender winds that kiss it and go by.
It shows a green full age: and what show I?
    A faded wrinkled face.

So often have I watched it, till mine eyes
Have filled with tears and I have ceased to see,
That now it seems a very friend to me,
    In all my secrets wise.

A faithful pleasant friend, who year by year
Grew with my growth and strengthened with my strength,
But whose green lifetime shows a longer length:
    When I shall not sit here

It still will bud in spring, and shed rare leaves
In autumn, and in summer-heat give shade,
And warmth in winter: when my bed is made
    In shade the cypress weaves.

Echo

Come to me in the silence of the night;
  Come in the speaking silence of a dream;
Come with soft rounded cheeks and eyes as bright
  As sunlight on a stream;
    Come back in tears,
O memory, hope, love of finished years.

O dream how sweet, too sweet, too bitter sweet,
  Whose wakening should have been in Paradise,
Where souls brimfull of love abide and meet;
  Where thirsting longing eyes
    Watch the slow door
That opening, letting in, lets out no more.

Yet come to me in dreams, that I may live
  My very life again though cold in death:
Come back to me in dreams, that I may give
  Pulse for pulse, breath for breath:
    Speak low, lean low,
As long ago, my love, how long ago.

from Sing-Song

An emerald is as green as grass;
  A ruby red as blood;
A sapphire shines as blue as heaven;
  A flint lies in the mud.

A diamond is a brilliant stone,
  To catch the world's desire;
An opal holds a fiery spark;
  But a flint holds fire.

'Endure hardness'

A cold wind stirs the blackthorn
    To burgeon and to blow,
Besprinkling half-green hedges
    With flakes and sprays of snow.

Through coldness and through keenness,
    Dear hearts, take comfort so:
Somewhere or other doubtless
    These make the blackthorn blow.

For Each

My harvest is done, its promise is ended,
    Weak and watery sets the sun,
Day and night in one mist are blended,
    My harvest is done.

    Long while running, how short when run,
Time to eternity has descended,
    Timeless eternity has begun.

Was it the narrow way that I wended?
    Snares and pits was it mine to shun?
The scythe has fallen, so long suspended,
    My harvest is done.

Goblin Market

Morning and evening
Maids heard the goblins cry:
'Come buy our orchard fruits,
Come buy, come buy:
Apples and quinces,
Lemons and oranges,
Plump unpecked cherries,
Melons and raspberries,
Bloom-down-cheeked peaches,
Swart-headed mulberries,
Wild free-born cranberries,
Crab-apples, dewberries,
Pine-apples, blackberries,
Apricots, strawberries;—
All ripe together
In summer weather,—
Morns that pass by,
Fair eves that fly;
Come buy, come buy:
Our grapes fresh from the vine,
Pomegranates full and fine,
Dates and sharp bullaces,
Rare pears and greengages,
Damsons and bilberries,
Taste them and try:
Currants and gooseberries,
Bright-fire-like barberries,
Figs to fill your mouth,
Citrons from the South,
Sweet to tongue and sound to eye;
Come buy, come buy.'

Evening by evening
Among the brookside rushes,
Laura bowed her head to hear,
Lizzie veiled her blushes:
Crouching close together

In the cooling weather,
With clasping arms and cautioning lips,
With tingling cheeks and finger tips.
'Lie close,' Laura said,
Pricking up her golden head:
'We must not look at goblin men,
We must not buy their fruits:
Who knows upon what soil they fed
Their hungry thirsty roots?'
'Come buy,' call the goblins
Hobbling down the glen.
'Oh,' cried Lizzie, 'Laura, Laura,
You should not peep at goblin men.'
Lizzie covered up her eyes,
Covered close lest they should look;
Laura reared her glossy head,
And whispered like the restless brook:
'Look, Lizzie, look, Lizzie,
Down the glen tramp little men.
One hauls a basket,
One bears a plate,
One lugs a golden dish
Of many pounds' weight.
How fair the vine must grow
Whose grapes are so luscious;
How warm the wind must blow
Through those fruit bushes.'
'No,' said Lizzie: 'No, no, no;
Their offers should not charm us,
Their evil gifts would harm us.'
She thrust a dimpled finger
In each ear, shut eyes and ran:
Curious Laura chose to linger
Wondering at each merchant man.
One had a cat's face,
One whisked a tail,
One tramped at a rat's pace,
One crawled like a snail,
One like a wombat prowled obtuse and furry,
One like a ratel tumbled hurry skurry.

She heard a voice like voice of doves
Cooing all together:
They sounded kind and full of loves
In the pleasant weather.

Laura stretched her gleaming neck
Like a rush-imbedded swan,
Like a lily from the beck,
Like a moonlit poplar branch,
Like a vessel at the launch
When its last restraint is gone.

Backwards up the mossy glen
Turned and trooped the goblin men,
With their shrill repeated cry,
'Come buy, come buy.'
When they reached where Laura was
They stood stock still upon the moss,
Leering at each other,
Brother with queer brother;
Signalling each other,
Brother with sly brother.
One set his basket down,
One reared his plate;
One began to weave a crown
Of tendrils, leaves, and rough nuts brown
(Men sell not such in any town);
One heaved the golden weight
Of dish and fruit to offer her:
'Come buy, come buy,' was still their cry.
Laura stared but did not stir,
Longed but had no money.
The whisk-tailed merchant bade her taste
In tones as smooth as honey,
The cat-faced purr'd,
The rat-paced spoke a word
Of welcome, and the snail-paced even was heard;
One parrot-voiced and jolly
Cried 'Pretty Goblin' still for 'Pretty Polly';
One whistled like a bird.

But sweet-tooth Laura spoke in haste:
'Good Folk, I have no coin;
To take were to purloin:
I have no copper in my purse,
I have no silver either,
And all my gold is on the furze
That shakes in windy weather
Above the rusty heather.'
'You have much gold upon your head,'
They answered all together:
'Buy from us with a golden curl.'
She clipped a precious golden lock,
She dropped a tear more rare than pearl,
Then sucked their fruit globes fair or red.
Sweeter than honey from the rock,
Stronger than man-rejoicing wine,
Clearer than water flowed that juice;
She never tasted such before,
How should it cloy with length of use?
She sucked and sucked and sucked the more
Fruits which that unknown orchard bore;
She sucked until her lips were sore;
Then flung the emptied rinds away
But gathered up one kernel stone,
And knew not was it night or day
As she turned home alone.

Lizzie met her at the gate
Full of wise upbraidings:
'Dear, you should not stay so late,
Twilight is not good for maidens;
Should not loiter in the glen
In the haunts of goblin men.
Do you not remember Jeanie,
How she met them in the moonlight,
Took their gifts both choice and many,
Ate their fruits and wore their flowers
Plucked from bowers
Where summer ripens at all hours?
But ever in the noonlight

She pined and pined away;
Sought them by night and day,
Found them no more, but dwindled and grew grey;
Then fell with the first snow,
While to this day no grass will grow
Where she lies low:
I planted daisies there a year ago
That never blow.
You should not loiter so.'
'Nay, hush,' said Laura:
'Nay, hush, my sister:
I ate and ate my fill,
Yet my mouth waters still:
Tomorrow night I will
Buy more'; and kissed her.
'Have done with sorrow;
I'll bring you plums tomorrow
Fresh on their mother twigs,
Cherries worth getting;
You cannot think what figs
My teeth have met in,
What melons icy-cold
Piled on a dish of gold
Too huge for me to hold,
What peaches with a velvet nap,
Pellucid grapes without one seed:
Odorous indeed must be the mead
Whereon they grow, and pure the wave they drink
With lilies at the brink,
And sugar-sweet their sap.'

Golden head by golden head,
Like two pigeons in one nest
Folded in each other's wings,
They lay down in their curtained bed:
Like two blossoms on one stem,
Like two flakes of new-fall'n snow,
Like two wands of ivory
Tipped with gold for awful kings.
Moon and stars gazed in at them,

Wind sang to them lullaby,
Lumbering owls forebore to fly,
Not a bat flapped to and fro
Round their rest:
Cheek to cheek and breast to breast
Locked together in one rest.

Early in the morning
When the first cock crowed his warning,
Neat like bees, as sweet and busy,
Laura rose with Lizzie:
Fetched in honey, milked the cows,
Aired and set to rights the house,
Kneaded cakes of whitest wheat,
Cakes for dainty mouths to eat,
Next churned butter, whipped up cream,
Fed their poultry, sat and sewed;
Talked as modest maidens should:
Lizzie with an open heart,
Laura in an absent dream,
One content, one sick in part;
One warbling for the mere bright day's delight,
One longing for the night.

At length slow evening came:
They went with pitchers to the reedy brook;
Lizzie most placid in her look,
Laura most like a leaping flame.
They drew the gurgling water from its deep.
Lizzie plucked purple and rich golden flags,
Then turning homeward said: 'The sunset flushes
Those furthest loftiest crags;
Come, Laura, not another maiden lags.
No wilful squirrel wags,
The beasts and birds are fast asleep.'
But Laura loitered still among the rushes,
And said the bank was steep.

And said the hour was early still,
The dew not fall'n, the wind not chill;
Listening ever, but not catching

The customary cry,
'Come buy, come buy,'
With its iterated jingle
Of sugar-baited words:
Not for all her watching
Once discerning even one goblin
Racing, whisking, tumbling, hobbling—
Let alone the herds
That used to tramp along the glen,
In groups or single,
Of brisk fruit-merchant men.

Till Lizzie urged, 'O Laura, come;
I hear the fruit-call, but I dare not look:
You should not loiter longer at this brook:
Come with me home.
The stars rise, the moon bends her arc,
Each glow-worm winks her spark,
Let us get home before the night grows dark:
For clouds may gather
Though this is summer weather,
Put out the lights and drench us through;
Then if we lost our way what should we do?'

Laura turned cold as stone
To find her sister heard that cry alone,
That goblin cry,
'Come buy our fruits, come buy.'
Must she then buy no more such dainty fruit?
Must she no more such succous pasture find,
Gone deaf and blind?
Her tree of life drooped from the root:
She said not one word in her heart's sore ache:
But peering thro' the dimness, nought discerning,
Trudged home, her pitcher dripping all the way;
So crept to bed, and lay
Silent till Lizzie slept;
Then sat up in a passionate yearning,
And gnashed her teeth for baulked desire, and wept
As if her heart would break.

Day after day, night after night,
Laura kept watch in vain
In sullen silence of exceeding pain.
She never caught again the goblin cry,
'Come buy, come buy';—
She never spied the goblin men
Hawking their fruits along the glen:
But when the noon waxed bright
Her hair grew thin and grey;
She dwindled, as the fair full moon doth turn
To swift decay and burn
Her fire away.

One day remembering her kernel-stone
She set it by a wall that faced the south;
Dewed it with tears, hoped for a root,
Watched for a waxing shoot,
But there came none.
It never saw the sun,
It never felt the trickling moisture run:
While with sunk eyes and faded mouth
She dreamed of melons, as a traveller sees
False waves in desert drouth
With shade of leaf-crowned trees,
And burns the thirstier in the sandful breeze.

She no more swept the house,
Tended the fowls or cows,
Fetched honey, kneaded cakes of wheat,
Brought water from the brook:
But sat down listless in the chimney-nook
And would not eat.

Tender Lizzie could not bear
To watch her sister's cankerous care,
Yet not to share.
She night and morning
Caught the goblins' cry:
'Come buy our orchard fruits,
Come buy, come buy:'—
Beside the brook, along the glen,

She heard the tramp of goblin men,
The voice and stir
Poor Laura could not hear;
Longed to buy fruit to comfort her,
But feared to pay too dear.
She thought of Jeanie in her grave,
Who should have been a bride;
But who for joys brides hope to have
Fell sick and died
In her gay prime,
In earliest winter time,
With the first glazing rime,
With the first snow-fall of crisp winter time.

Till Laura dwindling
Seemed knocking at Death's door.
Then Lizzie weighed no more
Better and worse;
But put a silver penny in her purse,
Kissed Laura, crossed the heath with clumps of furze
At twilight, halted by the brook:
And for the first time in her life
Began to listen and look.

Laughed every goblin
When they spied her peeping:
Came towards her hobbling,
Flying, running, leaping,
Puffing and blowing,
Chuckling, clapping, crowing,
Clucking and gobbling,
Mopping and mowing,
Full of airs and graces,
Pulling wry faces,
Demure grimaces,
Cat-like and rat-like,
Ratel- and wombat-like,
Snail-paced in a hurry,
Parrot-voiced and whistler,
Helter skelter, hurry skurry,

Chattering like magpies,
Fluttering like pigeons,
Gliding like fishes,—
Hugged her and kissed her:
Squeezed and caressed her:
Stretched up their dishes,
Panniers, and plates:
'Look at our apples
Russet and dun,
Bob at our cherries,
Bite at our peaches,
Citrons and dates,
Grapes for the asking,
Pears red with basking
Out in the sun,
Plums on their twigs;
Pluck them and suck them,—
Pomegranates, figs.'

'Good folk,' said Lizzie,
Mindful of Jeanie:
'Give me much and many:'
Held out her apron,
Tossed them her penny.
'Nay, take a seat with us,
Honour and eat with us,'
They answered grinning:
'Our feast is but beginning.
Night yet is early,
Warm and dew-pearly,
Wakeful and starry:
Such fruits as these
No man can carry;
Half their bloom would fly,
Half their dew would dry,
Half their flavour would pass by.
Sit down and feast with us,
Be welcome guest with us,
Cheer you and rest with us.'—
'Thank you,' said Lizzie: 'But one waits

At home alone for me:
So without further parleying,
If you will not sell me any
Of your fruits though much and many,
Give me back my silver penny
I tossed you for a fee.'—
They began to scratch their pates,
No longer wagging, purring,
But visibly demurring,
Grunting and snarling.
One called her proud,
Cross-grained, uncivil;
Their tones waxed loud,
Their looks were evil.
Lashing their tails
They trod and hustled her,
Elbowed and jostled her,
Clawed with their nails,
Barking, mewing, hissing, mocking,
Tore her gown and soiled her stocking,
Twitched her hair out by the roots,
Stamped upon her tender feet,
Held her hands and squeezed their fruits
Against her mouth to make her eat.

White and golden Lizzie stood,
Like a lily in a flood,—
Like a rock of blue-veined stone
Lashed by tides obstreperously,—
Like a beacon left alone
In a hoary roaring sea,
Sending up a golden fire,—
Like a fruit-crowned orange-tree
White with blossoms honey-sweet
Sore beset by wasp and bee,—
Like a royal virgin town
Topped with gilded dome and spire
Close beleaguered by a fleet
Mad to tug her standard down.

One may lead a horse to water,
Twenty cannot make him drink.
Though the goblins cuffed and caught her,
Coaxed and fought her,
Bullied and besought her,
Scratched her, pinched her black as ink,
Kicked and knocked her,
Mauled and mocked her,
Lizzie uttered not a word;
Would not open lip from lip
Lest they should cram a mouthful in:
But laughed in heart to feel the drip
Of juice that syruped all her face,
And lodged in dimples of her chin,
And streaked her neck which quaked like curd.
At last the evil people,
Worn out by her resistance,
Flung back her penny, kicked their fruit
Along whichever road they took,
Not leaving root or stone or shoot;
Some writhed into the ground,
Some dived into the brook
With ring and ripple,
Some scudded on the gale without a sound,
Some vanished in the distance.

In a smart, ache, tingle,
Lizzie went her way;
Knew not was it night or day;
Sprang up the bank, tore thro' the furze,
Threaded copse and dingle,
And heard her penny jingle
Bouncing in her purse,—
Its bounce was music to her ear.
She ran and ran
As if she feared some goblin man
Dogged her with gibe or curse
Or something worse:
But not one goblin skurried after,
Nor was she pricked by fear;

The kind heart made her windy-paced
That urged her home quite out of breath with haste
And inward laughter.

She cried, 'Laura,' up the garden.
'Did you miss me?
Come and kiss me.
Never mind my bruises,
Hug me, kiss me, suck my juices
Squeezed from goblin fruits for you,
Goblin pulp and goblin dew.
Eat me, drink me, love me;
Laura, make much of me;
For your sake I have braved the glen
And had to do with goblin merchant men.'

Laura started from her chair,
Flung her arms up in the air,
Clutched her hair:
'Lizzie, Lizzie, have you tasted
For my sake the fruit forbidden?
Must your light like mine be hidden,
Your young life like mine be wasted,
Undone in mine undoing,
And ruined in my ruin,
Thirsty, cankered, goblin-ridden?'—
She clung about her sister,
Kissed and kissed and kissed her:
Tears once again
Refreshed her shrunken eyes,
Dropping like rain
After long sultry drouth;
Shaking with aguish fear, and pain,
She kissed and kissed her with a hungry mouth.

Her lips began to scorch,
That juice was wormwood to her tongue,
She loathed the feast:
Writhing as one possessed she leaped and sung,
Rent all her robe, and wrung

Her hands in lamentable haste,
And beat her breast.
Her locks streamed like the torch
Borne by a racer at full speed,
Or like the mane of horses in their flight,
Or like an eagle when she stems the light
Straight toward the sun,
Or like a caged thing freed,
Or like a flying flag when armies run.

Swift fire spread through her veins, knocked at her heart
Met the fire smouldering there
And overbore its lesser flame;
She gorged on bitterness without a name:
Ah fool, to choose such part
Of soul-consuming care!
Sense failed in the mortal strife:
Like the watch-tower of a town
Which an earthquake shatters down,
Like a lightning-stricken mast,
Like a wind-uprooted tree
Spun about,
Like a foam-topped waterspout
Cast down headlong in the sea,
She fell at last;
Pleasure past and anguish past,
Is it death or is it life?

Life out of death.
That night long Lizzie watched by her,
Counted her pulse's flagging stir,
Felt for her breath,
Held water to her lips, and cooled her face
With tears and fanning leaves.
But when the first birds chirped about their eaves,
And early reapers plodded to the place
Of golden sheaves,
And dew-wet grass
Bowed in the morning winds so brisk to pass,

And new buds with new day
Opened of cup-like lilies on the stream,
Laura awoke as from a dream,
Laughed in the innocent old way,
Hugged Lizzie but not twice or thrice;
Her gleaming locks showed not one thread of grey,
Her breath was sweet as May,
And light danced in her eyes.

Days, weeks, months, years
Afterwards, when both were wives
With children of their own;
Their mother-hearts beset with fears,
Their lives bound up in tender lives;
Laura would call the little ones
And tell them of her early prime,
Those pleasant days long gone
Of not-returning time:
Would talk about the haunted glen,
The wicked quaint fruit-merchant men,
Their fruits like honey to the throat
But poison in the blood
(Men sell not such in any town):
Would tell them how her sister stood
In deadly peril to do her good,
And win the fiery antidote:
Then joining hands to little hands
Would bid them cling together,—
'For there is no friend like a sister
In calm or stormy weather;
To cheer one on the tedious way,
To fetch one if one goes astray,
To lift one if one totters down,
To strengthen whilst one stands.'

The Half Moon

The half moon shows a face of plaintive sweetness
    Ready and poised to wax or wane;
A fire of pale desire in incompleteness,
    Tending to pleasure or to pain:—
Lo, while we gaze she rolleth on in fleetness
    To perfect loss or perfect gain.

Half bitterness we know, we know half sweetness;
    This world is all on wax, on wane:
When shall completeness round time's incompleteness,
    Fulfilling joy, fulfilling pain?—
Lo, while we ask, life rolleth on in fleetness
    To finished loss or finished gain.

He and She

'Should one of us remember,
    And one of us forget,
I wish I knew what each will do—
    But who can tell as yet?'

'Should one of us remember,
    And one of us forget,
I promise you what I will do—
And I'm content to wait for you,
    And not be sure as yet.'

The Heart Knoweth
its own Bitterness

When all the over-work of life
 Is finished once, and fast asleep
We swerve no more beneath the knife
 But taste that silence cool and deep;
Forgetful of the highways rough,
 Forgetful of the thorny scourge,
 Forgetful of the tossing surge,
Then shall we find it is enough?

How can we say 'enough' on earth—
 'Enough' with such a craving heart?
I have not found it since my birth,
 But still have bartered part for part.
I have not held and hugged the whole,
 But paid the old to gain the new:
 Much have I paid, yet much is due,
Till I am beggared sense and soul.

I used to labour, used to strive
 For pleasure with a restless will:
Now if I save my soul alive
 All else what matters, good or ill?
I used to dream alone, to plan
 Unspoken hopes and days to come:—
 Of all my past this is the sum—
I will not lean on child of man.

To give, to give, not to receive!
 I long to pour myself, my soul,
Not to keep back or count or leave,
 But king with king to give the whole.
I long for one to stir my deep—
 I have had enough of help and gift—
 I long for one to search and sift
Myself, to take myself and keep.

You scratch my surface with your pin,
   You stroke me smooth with hushing breath:—
Nay pierce, nay probe, nay dig within,
   Probe my quick core and sound my depth.
You call me with a puny call,
   You talk, you smile, you nothing do:
   How should I spend my heart on you,
My heart that so outweighs you all?

Your vessels are by much too strait:
   Were I to pour, you could not hold.—
Bear with me: I must bear to wait,
   A fountain sealed through heat and cold.
Bear with me days or months or years:
   Deep must call deep until the end
   When friend shall no more envy friend
Nor vex his friend at unawares.

Not in this world of hope deferred,
   This world of perishable stuff:—
Eye hath not seen nor ear hath heard
   Nor heart conceived that full 'enough':
Here moans the separating sea,
   Here harvests fail, here breaks the heart:
   There God shall join and no man part,
I full of Christ and Christ of me.

Heaven Overarches

Heaven overarches earth and sea,
   Earth-sadness and sea-bitterness.
Heaven overarches you and me:
A little while and we shall be –
Please God – where there is no more sea
   Nor barren wilderness.

Heaven overarches you and me,
    And all earth's gardens and her graves.
Look up with me, until we see
The day break and the shadows flee.
What though tonight wrecks you and me
    If so tomorrow saves?

The Hour and the Ghost

BRIDE

O love, love, hold me fast,
He draws me away from thee;
I cannot stem the blast,
Nor the cold strong sea:
Far away a light shines
Beyond the hills and pines;
It is lit for me.

BRIDEGROOM

I have thee close, my dear,
No terror can come near;
Only far off the northern light shines clear.

GHOST

Come with me, fair and false,
To our home, come home.
It is my voice that calls:
Once thou wast not afraid
When I woo'd, and said,
'Come, our nest is newly made'—
Now cross the tossing foam.

BRIDE

Hold me one moment longer!
He taunts me with the past,
His clutch is waxing stronger;

Hold me fast, hold me fast.
He draws me from thy heart,
And I cannot withhold:
He bids my spirit depart
With him into the cold:—
Oh bitter vows of old!

BRIDEGROOM

Lean on me, hide thine eyes:
Only ourselves, earth and skies,
Are present here: be wise.

GHOST

Lean on me, come away,
I will guide and steady:
Come, for I will not stay:
Come, for house and bed are ready.
Ah sure bed and house,
For better and worse, for life and death,
Goal won with shortened breath!
Come, crown our vows.

BRIDE

One moment, one more word,
While my heart beats still,
While my breath is stirred
By my fainting will.
O friend, forsake me not,
Forget not as I forgot:
But keep thy heart for me,
Keep thy faith true and bright;
Through the lone cold winter night
Perhaps I may come to thee.

BRIDEGROOM

Nay peace, my darling, peace:
Let these dreams and terrors cease:
Who spoke of death or change or aught but ease?

GHOST

O fair frail sin,
O poor harvest gathered in!
Thou shalt visit him again
To watch his heart grow cold:
To know the gnawing pain
I knew of old;
To see one much more fair
Fill up the vacant chair,
Fill his heart, his children bear;
While thou and I together,
In the outcast weather,
Toss and howl and spin.

from Sing-Song

'I dreamt I caught a little owl
    And the bird was blue—'

  'But you may hunt for ever
And not find such an one.'

'I dreamt I set a sunflower,
    And red as blood it grew—'

  'But such a sunflower never
Bloomed beneath the sun.'

*

I dug and dug amongst the snow,
And thought the flowers would never grow;
I dug and dug amongst the sand,
And still no green thing came to hand.

Melt, O snow! the warm winds blow
To thaw the flowers and melt the snow;
But all the winds from every land
Will rear no blossom from the sand.

*

I planted a hand
    And there came up a palm,
I planted a heart
    And there came up balm.

Then I planted a wish,
    But there sprang a thorn,
While heaven frowned with thunder
    And earth sighed forlorn.

*

If a pig wore a wig,
    What could we say?
Treat him as a gentleman,
    And say 'Good day.'

If his tail chanced to fail,
    What could we do?—
Send him to the tailoress
    To get one new.

*

If hope grew on a bush,
    And joy grew on a tree,
What a nosegay for the plucking
    There would be!

But oh! in windy autumn,
    When frail flowers wither,

What should we do for hope and joy,
  Fading together?

from Songs for Strangers and Pilgrims

If love is not worth loving, then life is not worth living,
  Nor aught is worth remembering but well forgot;
For store is not worth storing and gifts are not worth giving,
  If love is not;

And idly cold is death-cold, and life-heat idly hot,
And vain is any offering and vainer our receiving,
  And vanity of vanities is all our lot.

Better than life's heaving heart is death's heart unheaving,
  Better than the opening leaves are the leaves that rot,
For there is nothing left worth achieving or retrieving,
  If love is not.

In an Artist's Studio

One face looks out from all his canvasses,
  One selfsame figure sits or walks or leans;
  We found her hidden just behind those screens,
That mirror gave back all her loveliness.
A queen in opal or in ruby dress,
  A nameless girl in freshest summer greens,
  A saint, an angel – every canvas means
The same one meaning, neither more nor less.
He feeds upon her face by day and night,
  And she with true kind eyes looks back on him,

Fair as the moon and joyful as the light:
  Not wan with waiting, not with sorrow dim;
Not as she is, but was when hope shone bright;
  Not as she is, but as she fills his dream.

Jessie Cameron

'Jessie, Jessie Cameron,
  Hear me but this once,' quoth he.
'Good luck go with you, neighbour's son,
  But I'm no mate for you,' quoth she.
Day was verging toward the night
  There beside the moaning sea:
Dimness overtook the light
  There where the breakers be.
'O Jessie, Jessie Cameron,
  I have loved you long and true.'—
'Good luck go with you, neighbour's son,
  But I'm no mate for you.'

She was a careless fearless girl,
  And made her answer plain,
Outspoken she to earl or churl,
  Kindhearted in the main,
But somewhat heedless with her tongue
  And apt at causing pain;
A mirthful maiden she and young,
  Most fair for bliss or bane.
'Oh long ago I told you so,
  I tell you so today:
Go you your way, and let me go
  Just my own free way.'

The sea swept in with moan and foam,
  Quickening the stretch of sand;
They stood almost in sight of home;

He strove to take her hand.
'Oh can't you take your answer then,
    And won't you understand?
For me you're not the man of men,
    I've other plans are planned.
You're good for Madge, or good for Cis,
    Or good for Kate, may be:
But what's to me the good of this
    While you're not good for me?'

They stood together on the beach,
    They two alone,
And louder waxed his urgent speech,
    His patience almost gone:
'Oh say but one kind word to me,
    Jessie, Jessie Cameron.'—
'I'd be too proud to beg,' quoth she,
    And pride was in her tone.
And pride was in her lifted head,
    And in her angry eye,
And in her foot, which might have fled
    But would not fly.

Some say that he had gipsy blood,
    That in his heart was guile:
Yet he had gone through fire and flood
    Only to win her smile.
Some say his grandam was a witch,
    A black witch from beyond the Nile,
Who kept an image in a niche
    And talked with it the while.
And by her hut far down the lane
    Some say they would not pass at night,
Lest they should hear an unked strain
    Or see an unked sight.

Alas for Jessie Cameron!—
    The sea crept moaning, moaning nigher;
She should have hastened to be gone,—
    The sea swept higher, breaking by her:—

She should have hastened to her home
    While yet the west was flushed with fire,—
But now her feet are in the foam,
    The sea-foam sweeping higher.
O mother, linger at your door,
    And light your lamp to make it plain;
But Jessie she comes home no more,
    No more again.

They stood together on the strand,
    They only each by each;
Home, her home, was close at hand,
    Utterly out of reach.
Her mother in the chimney nook
    Heard a startled sea-gull screech,
But never turned her head to look
    Towards the darkening beach:
Neighbours here and neighbours there
    Heard one scream, as if a bird
Shrilly screaming cleft the air:—
    That was all they heard.

Jessie she comes home no more,
    Comes home never;
Her lover's step sounds at his door
    No more for ever.
And boats may search upon the sea
    And search along the river,
But none know where the bodies be:
    Sea-winds that shiver,
Sea-birds that breast the blast,
    Sea-waves swelling,
Keep the secret first and last
    Of their dwelling.

Whether the tide so hemmed them round
    With its pitiless flow
That when they would have gone they found
    No way to go;
Whether she scorned him to the last

With words flung to and fro,
Or clung to him when hope was past,
   None will ever know:
Whether he helped or hindered her,
   Threw up his life or lost it well,
The troubled sea for all its stir
   Finds no voice to tell.

Only watchers by the dying
   Have thought they heard one pray
Wordless, urgent; and replying
   One seem to say him nay:
And watchers by the dead have heard
   A windy swell from miles away,
With sobs and screams, but not a word
   Distinct for them to say:
And watchers out at sea have caught
   Glimpse of a pale gleam here or there,
Come and gone as quick as thought,
   Which might be hand or hair.

'Judge not according to the appearance'

Lord, purge our eyes to see
Within the seed a tree,
   Within the glowing egg a bird,
    Within the shroud a butterfly:

Till taught by such, we see
Beyond all creatures Thee,
   And hearken for Thy tender word,
    And hear it, 'Fear not: it is I.'

from Sing-Song

'Kookoorookoo! kookoorookoo!'
　Crows the cock before the morn;
'Kikirikee! kikirikee!'
　Roses in the east are born.

'Kookoorookoo! kookoorookoo!'
　Early birds begin their singing;
'Kikirikee! kikirikee!'
　The day, the day, the day is springing.

*

Lie a-bed,
Sleepy head,
Shut up eyes, bo-peep;
Till daybreak
Never wake:—
Baby, sleep.

L. E. L.

'Whose heart was breaking for a little love.'

Downstairs I laugh, I sport and jest with all;
　But in my solitary room above
I turn my face in silence to the wall;
　My heart is breaking for a little love
　　Though winter frosts are done,
　　And birds pair every one,
And leaves peep out, for springtide is begun.

I feel no spring, while spring is well-nigh blown,
　I find no nest, while nests are in the grove:
Woe's me for mine own heart that dwells alone,

My heart that breaketh for a little love.
   While golden in the sun
   Rivulets rise and run,
While lilies bud, for springtide is begun.

All love, are loved, save only I; their hearts
  Beat warm with love and joy, beat full thereof:
They cannot guess, who play the pleasant parts,
  My heart is breaking for a little love.
   While bee-hives wake and whirr,
   And rabbit thins his fur,
In living spring that sets the world astir.

I deck myself with silks and jewelry,
  I plume myself like any mated dove:
They praise my rustling show, and never see
  My heart is breaking for a little love.
   While sprouts green lavender
   With rosemary and myrrh,
For in quick spring the sap is all astir.

Perhaps some saints in glory guess the truth,
  Perhaps some angels read it as they move,
And cry one to another full of ruth,
  'Her heart is breaking for a little love.'
   Though other things have birth,
   And leap and sing for mirth,
When springtime wakes and clothes and feeds the earth.

Yet saith a saint, 'Take patience for thy scathe';
  Yet saith an angel: 'Wait, and thou shalt prove
True best is last, true life is born of death,
  O thou, heart-broken for a little love.
   Then love shall fill thy girth,
   And love make fat thy dearth,
When new spring builds new heaven and clean new earth.'

A Life's Parallels

Never on this side of the grave again,
　On this side of the river,
On this side of the garner of the grain,
　　Never,—

Ever while time flows on and on and on,
　That narrow noiseless river,
Ever while corn bows heavy-headed, wan,
　　Ever,—

Never despairing, often fainting, rueing,
　But looking back, ah never!
Faint yet pursuing, faint yet still pursuing
　　Ever.

Looking Back

Looking back along life's trodden way
　Gleams and greenness linger on the track;
Distance melts and mellows all today,
　　Looking back.

Rose and purple and a silvery grey,
　Is that cloud the cloud we called so black?
Evening harmonizes all today,
　　Looking back.

Foolish feet so prone to halt or stray,
　Foolish heart so restive on the rack!
Yesterday we sighed, but not today
　　Looking back.

O Lord, when Thou didst call me

O Lord, when Thou didst call me, didst Thou know
  My heart disheartened through and through,
  Still hankering after Egypt full in view
Where cucumbers and melons grow?
          —'Yea, I knew.'—

But, Lord, when Thou didst choose me, didst Thou know
  How marred I was and withered too,
  Nor rose for sweetness nor for virtue rue,
Timid and rash, hasty and slow?
          —'Yea, I knew.'—

My Lord, when Thou didst love me, didst Thou know
  How weak my efforts were, how few,
  Tepid to love and impotent to do,
Envious to reap while slack to sow?
          —'Yea, I knew.'—

Good Lord, Who knowest what I cannot know
  And dare not know, my false, my true,
  My new, my old; Good Lord, arise and do
Where cucumbers anknown me so.
          —'Yea, I knew.'—

Love from the North

I had a love in soft south land,
  Beloved through April far in May;
He waited on my lightest breath,
  And never dared to say me nay.

He saddened if my cheer was sad,
    But gay he grew if I was gay;
We never differed on a hair,
    My yes his yes, my nay his nay.

The wedding hour was come, the aisles
    Were flushed with sun and flowers that day;
I pacing balanced in my thoughts:
    'It's quite too late to think of nay.'—

My bridegroom answered in his turn,
    Myself had almost answered 'yea';
When through the flashing nave I heard
    A struggle and resounding 'nay'.

Bridemaids and bridegroom shrank in fear,
    But I stood high who stood at bay:
'And if I answer yea, fair Sir,
    What man art thou to bar with nay?'

He was a strong man from the north,
    Light-locked, with eyes of dangerous grey:
'Put yea by for another time
    In which I will not say thee nay.'

He took me in his strong white arms,
    He bore me on his horse away
O'er crag, morass, and hairbreadth pass,
    But never asked me yea or nay.

He made me fast with book and bell,
    With links of love he makes me stay;
Till now I've neither heart nor power
    Nor will nor wish to say him nay.

The Lowest Place

Give me the lowest place; not that I dare
   Ask for that lowest place, but Thou hast died
That I might live and share
   Thy glory by Thy side.

Give me the lowest place: or if for me
   That lowest place too high, make one more low
Where I may sit and see
   My God and love Thee so.

Maude Clare

Out of the church she followed them
   With a lofty step and mien:
His bride was like a village maid,
   Maude Clare was like a queen.
'Son Thomas,' his lady mother said,
   With smiles, almost with tears:
'May Nell and you but live as true
   As we have done for years;

'Your father thirty years ago
   Had just your tale to tell;
But he was not so pale as you,
   Nor I so pale as Nell.'

My lord was pale with inward strife,
   And Nell was pale with pride;
My lord gazed long on pale Maude Clare
   Or ever he kissed the bride.

'Lo, I have brought my gift, my lord,
  Have brought my gift,' she said:
'To bless the hearth, to bless the board,
  To bless the marriage-bed.

'Here's my half of the golden chain
  You wore about your neck,
That day we waded ankle-deep
  For lilies in the beck.

'Here's my half of the faded leaves
  We plucked from budding bough,
With feet amongst the lily leaves,—
  The lilies are budding now.'

He strove to match her scorn with scorn,
  He faltered in his place:
'Lady,' he said, – 'Maude Clare,' he said,—
  'Maude Clare': – and hid his face.

She turned to Nell: 'My Lady Nell,
  I have a gift for you;
Though, were it fruit, the bloom were gone,
  Or, were it flowers, the dew.

'Take my share of a fickle heart,
  Mine of a paltry love:
Take it or leave it as you will,
  I wash my hands thereof.'

'And what you leave,' said Nell, 'I'll take,
  And what you spurn I'll wear;
For he's my lord for better and worse,
  And him I love, Maude Clare.

'Yea though you're taller by the head,
  More wise, and much more fair,
I'll love him till he loves me best—
  Me best of all, Maude Clare.'

Memory

1

I nursed it in my bosom while it lived,
  I hid it in my heart when it was dead.
In joy I sat alone; even so I grieved
    Alone, and nothing said.

I shut the door to face the naked truth,
  I stood alone – I faced the truth alone,
Stripped bare of self-regard or forms or ruth
    Till first and last were shown.

I took the perfect balances and weighed;
  No shaking of my hand disturbed the poise;
Weighed, found it wanting: not a word I said,
    But silent made my choice.

None know the choice I made; I make it still.
  None know the choice I made and broke my heart,
Breaking mine idol: I have braced my will
    Once, chosen for once my part.

I broke it at a blow, I laid it cold,
  Crushed in my deep heart where it used to live.
My heart dies inch by inch; the time grows old,
    Grows old in which I grieve.

2

I have a room whereinto no one enters
  Save I myself alone:
  There sits a blessed memory on a throne,
There my life centres;

While winter comes and goes – oh tedious comer!—
  And while its nip-wind blows;

While bloom the bloodless lily and warm rose
Of lavish summer.

If any should force entrance he might see there
   One buried yet not dead,
   Before whose face I no more bow my head
Or bend my knee there;

But often in my worn life's autumn weather
   I watch there with clear eyes,
   And think how it will be in Paradise
When we're together.

Mirage

The hope I dreamed of was a dream,
   Was but a dream; and now I wake,
Exceeding comfortless, and worn, and old,
   For a dream's sake.

I hang my harp upon a tree,
   A weeping willow in a lake;
I hang my silenced harp there, wrung and snapt
   For a dream's sake.

Lie still, lie still, my breaking heart;
   My silent heart, lie still and break:
Life, and the world, and mine own self, are changed
   For a dream's sake.

Monna Innominata

A SONNET OF SONNETS

Beatrice, immortalized by 'altissimo poeta ... cotanto amante'; Laura, celebrated by a great though an inferior bard, – have alike paid the exceptional penalty of exceptional honour, and have come down to us resplendent with charms, but (at least, to my apprehension) scant of attractiveness.

These heroines of world-wide fame were preceded by a bevy of unnamed ladies, 'donne innominate', sung by a school of less conspicuous poets; and in that land and that period which gave simultaneous birth to Catholics, to Albigenses, and to Troubadours, one can imagine many a lady as sharing her lover's poetic aptitude, while the barrier between them might be one held sacred by both, yet not such as to render mutual love incompatible with mutual honour.

Had such a lady spoken for herself, the portrait left us might have appeared more tender, if less dignified, than any drawn even by a devoted friend. Or had the Great Poetess of our own day and nation only been unhappy instead of happy, her circumstances would have invited her to bequeath to us, in lieu of the 'Portuguese Sonnets', an inimitable 'donna innominata' drawn not from fancy but from feeling, and worthy to occupy a niche beside Beatrice and Laura.

1

'Lo dì che han detto a' dolci amici addio.'—DANTE
'Amor, con quanto sforzo oggi mi vinci!'—PETRARCA

Come back to me, who wait and watch for you:—
    Or come not yet, for it is over then,
    And long it is before you come again,
So far between my pleasures are and few.
While, when you come not, what I do I do
    Thinking 'Now when he comes', my sweetest 'when':
    For one man is my world of all the men
This wide world holds; O love, my world is you.
Howbeit, to meet you grows almost a pang
    Because the pang of parting comes so soon;
    My hope hangs waning, waxing, like a moon
Between the heavenly days on which we meet:

Ah me, but where are now the songs I sang
    When life was sweet because you called them sweet?

2

'Era già l'ora che volge il desio.'—DANTE
'Ricorro al tempo ch' io vi vidi prima.'—PETRARCA

I wish I could remember that first day,
    First hour, first moment of your meeting me,
    If bright or dim the season, it might be
Summer or Winter for aught I can say;
So unrecorded did it slip away,
    So blind was I to see and to foresee,
    So dull to mark the budding of my tree
That would not blossom yet for many a May.
If only I could recollect it, such
    A day of days! I let it come and go
    As traceless as a thaw of bygone snow;
It seemed to mean so little, meant so much;
If only now I could recall that touch,
    First touch of hand in hand – Did one but know!

3

'O ombre vane, fuor che ne l'aspetto!' —DANTE
'Immaginata guida la conduce.'—PETRARCA

I dream of you, to wake: would that I might
    Dream of you and not wake but slumber on;
    Nor find with dreams the dear companion gone,
As, Summer ended, Summer birds take flight.
In happy dreams I hold you full in sight,
    I blush again who waking look so wan;
    Brighter than sunniest day that ever shone,
In happy dreams your smile makes day of night.
Thus only in a dream we are at one,
    Thus only in a dream we give and take
        The faith that maketh rich who take or give;
    If thus to sleep is sweeter than to wake,
        To die were surely sweeter than to live,
Though there be nothing new beneath the sun.

4

'Poca favilla gran fiamma seconda.'—DANTE
'Ogni altra cosa, ogni pensier va fore,
E sol ivi con voi rimansi amore.'—PETRARCA

I loved you first: but afterwards your love,
   Outsoaring mine, sang such a loftier song
As drowned the friendly cooings of my dove.
   Which owes the other most? My love was long,
   And yours one moment seemed to wax more strong;
I loved and guessed at you, you construed me
And loved me for what might or might not be—
   Nay, weights and measures do us both a wrong.
For verily love knows not 'mine' or 'thine';
   With separate 'I' and 'thou' free love has done,
     For one is both and both are one in love:
Rich love knows nought of 'thine that is not mine';
     Both have the strength and both the length thereof,
Both of us, of the love which makes us one.

5

'Amor che a nullo amato amar perdona.'—DANTE
'Amor m'addusse in sì gioiosa spene.'—PETRARCA

O my heart's heart, and you who are to me
   More than myself myself, God be with you,
   Keep you in strong obedience leal and true
To Him whose noble service setteth free;
Give you all good we see or can foresee,
   Make your joys many and your sorrows few,
   Bless you in what you bear and what you do,
Yea, perfect you as He would have you be.
So much for you; but what for me, dear friend?
   To love you without stint and all I can,
Today, tomorrow, world without an end;
To love you much and yet to love you more,
   As Jordan at his flood sweeps either shore;
   Since woman is the helpmeet made for man.

6

'Or puoi la quantitate
Comprender de l'amor che a te mi scalda.'—DANTE
'Non vo' che da tal nodo amor mi scioglia.'—PETRARCA

Trust me, I have not earned your dear rebuke—
   I love, as you would have me, God the most;
   Would lose not Him, but you, must one be lost,
Nor with Lot's wife cast back a faithless look,
Unready to forego what I forsook;
   This say I, having counted up the cost,
   This, though I be the feeblest of God's host,
The sorriest sheep Christ shepherds with His crook.
Yet while I love my God the most, I deem
   That I can never love you over-much;
     I love Him more, so let me love you too;
   Yea, as I apprehend it, love is such
I cannot love you if I love not Him,
     I cannot love Him if I love not you.

7

'Qui primavera sempre ed ogni frutto.'—DANTE
'Ragionando con meco ed io con lui.'—PETRARCA

'Love me, for I love you' – and answer me,
   'Love me, for I love you': so shall we stand
   As happy equals in the flowering land
Of love, that knows not a dividing sea.
   Love builds the house on rock and not on sand,
Love laughs what while the winds rave desperately;
   And who hath found love's citadel unmanned?
And who hath held in bonds love's liberty?—
My heart's a coward though my words are brave—
   We meet so seldom, yet we surely part
   So often; there's a problem for your art!
   Still I find comfort in his Book who saith,
Though jealousy be cruel as the grave,
   And death be strong, yet love is strong as death.

8

'Come dicesse a Dio, D'altro non calme.'—DANTE
'Spero trovar pietà non che perdono.'—PETRARCA

'I, if I perish, perish' – Esther spake:
   And bride of life or death she made her fair
   In all the lustre of her perfumed hair
And smiles that kindle longing but to slake.
She put on pomp of loveliness, to take
   Her husband through his eyes at unaware;
   She spread abroad her beauty for a snare,
Harmless as doves and subtle as a snake.
She trapped him with one mesh of silken hair,
   She vanquished him by wisdom of her wit,
     And built her people's house that it should stand:—
     If I might take my life so in my hand,
And for my love to Love put up my prayer,
   And for love's sake by Love be granted it!

9

'O dignitosa coscienza e netta!'—DANTE
'Spirto più acceso di virtuti ardenti.'—PETRARCA

Thinking of you, and all that was, and all
   That might have been and now can never be,
   I feel your honoured excellence, and see
Myself unworthy of the happier call:
For woe is me who walk so apt to fall,
   So apt to shrink afraid, so apt to flee,
   Apt to lie down and die (ah woe is me!)
Faithless and hopeless turning to the wall.
And yet not hopeless quite nor faithless quite,
Because not loveless; love may toil all night,
But take at morning; wrestle till the break
   Of day, but then wield power with God and man:
   So take I heart of grace as best I can,
Ready to spend and be spent for your sake.

10

'Con miglior corso e con migliore stella.'—DANTE
'La vita fugge e non s'arresta un' ora.'—PETRARCA

Time flies, hope flags, life plies a wearied wing;
 Death following hard on life gains ground apace;
 Faith runs with each and rears an eager face,
Outruns the rest, makes light of everything,
Spurns earth, and still finds breath to pray and sing;
 While love ahead of all uplifts his praise,
 Still asks for grace and still gives thanks for grace,
Content with all day brings and night will bring.
Life wanes; and when love folds his wings above
 Tired hope, and less we feel his conscious pulse,
  Let us go fall asleep, dear friend, in peace:
  A little while, and age and sorrow cease;
 A little while, and life reborn annuls
Loss and decay and death, and all is love.

11

'Vien dietro a me e lascia dir le genti.'—DANTE
'Contando i casi della vita nostra.'—PETRARCA

Many in aftertimes will say of you
 'He loved her' – while of me what will they say?
 Not that I loved you more than just in play,
For fashion's sake as idle women do.
Even let them prate; who know not what we knew
 Of love and parting in exceeding pain,
 Of parting hopeless here to meet again,
Hopeless on earth, and heaven is out of view.
But by my heart of love laid bare to you,
 My love that you can make not void nor vain,
Love that foregoes you but to claim anew
Beyond this passage of the gate of death,
 I charge you at the Judgment make it plain
My love of you was life and not a breath.

12

'Amor che ne la mente mi ragiona.'—DANTE
'Amor vien nel bel viso di costei.'—PETRARCA

If there be any one can take my place
   And make you happy whom I grieve to grieve,
   Think not that I can grudge it, but believe
I do commend you to that nobler grace,
That readier wit than mine, that sweeter face;
   Yea, since your riches make me rich, conceive
   I too am crowned while bridal crowns I weave,
And thread the bridal dance with jocund pace.
For if I did not love you, it might be
   That I should grudge you some one dear delight;
     But since the heart is yours that was mine own,
   Your pleasure is my pleasure, right my right,
Your honourable freedom makes me free,
     And you companioned I am not alone.

13

'E drizzeremo glí occhi al Primo Amore.'—DANTE
'Ma trovo peso non da le mie braccia.'—PETRARCA

If I could trust mine own self with your fate,
   Shall I not rather trust it in God's hand?
   Without Whose Will one lily doth not stand,
Nor sparrow fall at his appointed date;
   Who numbereth the innumerable sand,
Who weighs the wind and water with a weight,
To Whom the world is neither small nor great,
   Whose knowledge foreknew every plan we planned.
Searching my heart for all that touches you,
   I find there only love and love's goodwill
Helpless to help and impotent to do,
Of understanding dull, of sight most dim;
And therefore I commend you back to Him
   Whose love your love's capacity can fill.

14

'E la Sua Volontade è nostra pace.'—DANTE
'Sol con questi pensier, con altre chiome.'—PETRARCA

Youth gone, and beauty gone if ever there
   Dwelt beauty in so poor a face as this;
     Youth gone and beauty, what remains of bliss?
I will not bind fresh roses in my hair,
To shame a cheek at best but little fair,—
     Leave youth his roses, who can bear a thorn,—
I will not seek for blossoms anywhere,
     Except such common flowers as blow with corn.
Youth gone and beauty gone, what doth remain?
   The longing of a heart pent up forlorn,
      A silent heart whose silence loves and longs;
      The silence of a heart which sang its songs
     While youth and beauty made a summer morn,
Silence of love that cannot sing again.

My Dream

Hear now a curious dream I dreamed last night,
Each word whereof is weighed and sifted truth.

I stood beside Euphrates while it swelled
Like overflowing Jordan in its youth.
It waxed and coloured sensibly to sight;
Till out of myriad pregnant waves there welled
Young crocodiles, a gaunt blunt-featured crew,
Fresh-hatched perhaps and daubed with birthday dew.
The rest if I should tell, I fear my friend,
My closest friend, would deem the facts untrue;
And therefore it were wisely left untold;
Yet if you will, why, hear it to the end.

Each crocodile was girt with massive gold
And polished stones that with their wearers grew:

But one there was who waxed beyond the rest,
Wore kinglier girdle and a kingly crown,
Whilst crowns and orbs and sceptres starred his breast.
All gleamed compact and green with scale on scale,
But special burnishment adorned his mail
And special terror weighed upon his frown;
His punier brethren quaked before his tail,
Broad as a rafter, potent as a flail.
So he grew lord and master of his kin:
But who shall tell the tale of all their woes?
An execrable appetite arose,
He battened on them, crunched, and sucked them in.
He knew no law, he feared no binding law,
But ground them with inexorable jaw.
The luscious fat distilled upon his chin,
Exuded from his nostrils and his eyes,
While still like hungry death he fed his maw;
Till, every minor crocodile being dead
And buried too, himself gorged to the full,
He slept with breath oppressed and unstrung claw.

Oh marvel passing strange which next I saw!
In sleep he dwindled to the common size,
And all the empire faded from his coat.
Then from far off a wingèd vessel came,
Swift as a swallow, subtle as a flame:
I know not what it bore of freight or host,
But white it was as an avenging ghost.
It levelled strong Euphrates in its course;
Supreme yet weightless as an idle mote
It seemed to tame the waters without force
Till not a murmur swelled or billow beat.
Lo, as the purple shadow swept the sands,
The prudent crocodile rose on his feet,
And shed appropriate tears and wrung his hands.

What can it mean? you ask. I answer not
For meaning, but myself must echo, What?
And tell it as I saw it on the spot.

'No, Thank You, John'

I never said I loved you, John:
   Why will you teaze me day by day,
And wax a weariness to think upon
    With always 'do' and 'pray'?

You know I never loved you, John;
   No fault of mine made me your toast:
Why will you haunt me with a face as wan
    As shows an hour-old ghost?

I dare say Meg or Moll would take
   Pity upon you, if you'd ask:
And pray don't remain single for my sake
    Who can't perform that task.

I have no heart? – Perhaps I have not;
   But then you're mad to take offence
That I don't give you what I have not got:
    Use your own common sense.

Let bygones be bygones:
   Don't call me false, who owed not to be true:
I'd rather answer 'No' to fifty Johns
    Than answer 'Yes' to you.

Let's mar our pleasant days no more,
   Song-birds of passage, days of youth:
Catch at today, forget the days before:
    I'll wink at your untruth.

Let us strike hands as hearty friends;
   No more, no less; and friendship's good:
Only don't keep in view ulterior ends,
    And points not understood

In open treaty. Rise above
  Quibbles and shuffling off and on:
Here's friendship for you if you like; but love,—
  No, thank you, John.

Noble Sisters

'Now did you mark a falcon,
  Sister dear, sister dear,
Flying toward my window
  In the morning cool and clear?
With jingling bells about her neck,
  But what beneath her wing?
It may have been a ribbon,
  Or it may have been a ring.'—
    'I marked a falcon swooping
      At the break of day:
    And for your love, my sister dove,
      I 'frayed the thief away.'—

'Or did you spy a ruddy hound,
  Sister fair and tall,
Went snuffing round my garden bound,
  Or crouched by my bower wall?
With a silken leash about his neck
  But in his mouth may be
A chain of gold and silver links,
  Or a letter writ to me.'—
    'I heard a hound, highborn sister,
      Stood baying at the moon:
    I rose and drove him from your wall
      Lest you should wake too soon.'—

'Or did you meet a pretty page
  Sat swinging on the gate?

Sat whistling whistling like a bird,
   Or may be slept too late:
With eaglets broidered on his cap,
   And eaglets on his glove.
If you had turned his pockets out,
   You had found some pledge of love.'—
      'I met him at this daybreak,
        Scarce the east was red:
      Lest the creaking gate should anger you
        I packed him home to bed.'—

'O patience, sister! Did you see
   A young man tall and strong,
Swift-footed to uphold the right
   And to uproot the wrong,
Come home across the desolate sea
   To woo me for his wife?
And in his heart my heart is locked,
   And in his life my life.'—
      'I met a nameless man, sister,
        Who loitered round our door:
      I said: Her husband loves her much
        And yet she loves him more.'—

'Fie, sister, fie, a wicked lie!
   A lie, a wicked lie!
I have none other love but him,
   Nor will have till I die.
And you have turned him from our door,
   And stabbed him with a lie:
I will go seek him through the world
   In sorrow till I die.'—
      'Go seek in sorrow, sister,
        And find in sorrow too:
      If thus you shame our father's name
        My curse go forth with you.'

On the Wing

Once in a dream (for once I dreamed of you)
    We stood together in an open field;
    Above our heads two swift-winged pigeons wheeled,
Sporting at ease and courting full in view:—
When loftier still a broadening darkness flew,
    Down-swooping, and a ravenous hawk revealed;
    Too weak to fight, too fond to fly, they yield;
So farewell life and love and pleasures new.
Then as their plumes fell fluttering to the ground,
    Their snow-white plumage flecked with crimson drops,
        I wept, and thought I turned towards you to weep:
    But you were gone; while rustling hedgerow tops
Bent in a wind which bore to me a sound
        Of far-off piteous bleat of lambs and sheep.

Parting

Parting after parting,
    Sore loss and gnawing pain:
Meeting grows half a sorrow
    Because of parting again.
When shall the day break
    That these things shall not be?
When shall new earth be ours
    Without a sea,
And time that is not time
    But eternity?

To meet, worth living for;
  Worth dying for, to meet;
To meet, worth parting for,
  Bitter forgot in sweet:
To meet, worth parting before,
  Never to part more.

Promises like Piecrust

Promise me no promises,
  So will I not promise you;
Keep we both our liberties,
  Never false and never true:
Let us hold the die uncast,
  Free to come as free to go;
For I cannot know your past,
  And of mine what can you know?

You, so warm, may once have been
  Warmer towards another one;
I, so cold, may once have seen
  Sunlight, once have felt the sun:
Who shall show us if it was
  Thus indeed in time of old?
Fades the image from the glass
  And the fortune is not told.

If you promised, you might grieve
  For lost liberty again;
If I promised, I believe
  I should fret to break the chain:
Let us be the friends we were,
  Nothing more but nothing less;
Many thrive on frugal fare
  Who would perish of excess.

The Queen of Hearts

How comes it, Flora, that, whenever we
Play cards together, you invariably,
    However the pack parts,
    Still hold the Queen of Hearts?

I've scanned you with a scrutinizing gaze,
Resolved to fathom these your secret ways:
    But, sift them as I will,
    Your ways are secret still.

I cut and shuffle; shuffle, cut, again;
But all my cutting, shuffling, proves in vain:
    Vain hope, vain forethought too;
    That Queen still falls to you.

I dropped her once, prepense; but, ere the deal
Was dealt, your instinct seemed her loss to feel:
    'There should be one card more,'
    You said, and searched the floor.

I cheated once; I made a private notch
In Heart-Queen's back, and kept a lynx-eyed watch;
    Yet such another back
    Deceived me in the pack:

The Queen of Clubs assumed by arts unknown
An imitative dint that seemed my own;
    This notch, not of my doing,
    Misled me to my ruin.

It baffles me to puzzle out the clue,
Which must be skill, or craft, or luck in you:
    Unless, indeed, it be
    Natural affinity.

Remember

Remember me when I am gone away,
   Gone far away into the silent land;
   When you can no more hold me by the hand.
Nor I half turn to go yet turning stay.
Remember me when no more day by day
   You tell me of our future that you plann'd:
   Only remember me; you understand
It will be late to counsel then or pray.
Yet if you should forget me for a while
   And afterwards remember, do not grieve:
   For if the darkness and corruption leave
   A vestige of the thoughts that once I had,
Better by far you should forget and smile
   Than that you should remember and be sad.

Roses on a Brier

Roses on a brier,
   Pearls from out the bitter sea,
Such is earth's desire
   However pure it be.

Neither bud nor brier,
   Neither pearl nor brine for me:
Be stilled, my long desire;
   There shall be no more sea.

Be stilled, my passionate heart;
   Old earth shall end, new earth shall be:
Be still, and earn thy part
   Where shall be no more sea.

A Royal Princess

I a Princess king-descended, deckt with jewels, gilded, drest,
Would rather be a peasant with her baby at her breast,
For all I shine so like the sun, and am purple like the west.

Two and two my guards behind, two and two before,
Two and two on either hand, they guard me evermore:
Me, poor dove that must not coo – eagle that must not soar.

All my fountains cast up perfumes, all my gardens grow
Scented woods and foreign spices, with all flowers in blow
That are costly, out of season as the seasons go.

All my walls are lost in mirrors, whereupon I trace
Self to right hand, self to left hand, self in every place,
Self-same solitary figure, self-same seeking face.

Then I have an ivory chair high to sit upon,
Almost like my father's chair which is an ivory throne;
There I sit uplift and upright, there I sit alone,

Alone by day, alone by night, alone days without end;
My father and my mother give me treasures, search and spend—
O my father! O my mother! have you ne'er a friend?

As I am a lofty princess, so my father is
A lofty king, accomplished in all kingly subtilties,
Holding in his strong right hand world-kingdoms' balances.

He has quarrelled with his neighbours, he has scourged his foes;
Vassal counts and princes follow where his pennon goes,
Long-descended valiant lords whom the vulture knows,

On whose track the vulture swoops, when they ride in state
To break the strength of armies and topple down the great:
Each of these my courteous servant, none of these my mate.

My father counting up his strength sets down with equal pen
So many head of cattle, head of horses, head of men;
These for slaughter, these for labour, with the how and when.

Some to work on roads, canals; some to man his ships;
Some to smart in mines beneath sharp overseers' whips;
Some to trap fur-beasts in lands where utmost winter nips.

Once it came into my heart, and whelmed me like a flood,
That these too are men and women, human flesh and blood;
Men with hearts and men with souls, though trodden down like
    mud.

Our feasting was not glad that night, our music was not gay:
On my mother's graceful head I marked a thread of grey,
My father frowning at the fare seemed every dish to weigh.

I sat beside them sole princess in my exalted place,
My ladies and my gentlemen stood by me on the dais:
A mirror showed me I look old and haggard in the face;

It showed me that my ladies all are fair to gaze upon,
Plump, plenteous-haired, to every one love's secret lore is known,
They laugh by day, they sleep by night; ah me, what is a throne?

The singing men and women sang that night as usual,
The dancers danced in pairs and sets, but music had a fall,
A melancholy windy fall as at a funeral.

Amid the toss of torches to my chamber back we swept;
My ladies loosed my golden chain; meantime I could have wept
To think of some in galling chains whether they waked or slept.

I took my bath of scented milk, delicately waited on:
They burned sweet things for my delight, cedar and cinnamon,
They lit my shaded silver lamp, and left me there alone.

A day went by, a week went by. One day I heard it said:
'Men are clamouring, women, children, clamouring to be fed;
Men like famished dogs are howling in the streets for bread.'

So two whispered by my door, not thinking I could hear,
Vulgar naked truth, ungarnished for a royal ear;
Fit for cooping in the background, not to stalk so near.

But I strained my utmost sense to catch this truth, and mark:
'There are families out grazing, like cattle in the park.'
'A pair of peasants must be saved, even if we build an ark.'

A merry jest, a merry laugh: each strolled upon his way;
One was my page, a lad I reared and bore with day by day;
One was my youngest maid, as sweet and white as cream in
May.

Other footsteps followed softly with a weightier tramp;
Voices said: 'Picked soldiers have been summoned from the
camp,
To quell these base-born ruffians who make free to howl and
stamp.'

'Howl and stamp?' one answered: 'They made free to hurl a
stone
At the minister's state coach, well aimed and stoutly thrown.'
'There's work then for the soldiers, for this rank crop must be
mown.'

'One I saw, a poor old fool with ashes on his head,
Whimpering because a girl had snatched his crust of bread:
Then he dropped; when some one raised him, it turned out he was
dead.'

'After us the deluge,' was retorted with a laugh:
'If bread's the staff of life they must walk without a staff.'
'While I've a loaf they're welcome to my blessing and the chaff.'

These passed. 'The king': stand up. Said my father with a smile:
'Daughter mine, your mother comes to sit with you awhile;
She's sad today, and who but you her sadness can beguile?'

He too left me. Shall I touch my harp now while I wait,—
(I hear them doubling guard below before our palace gate)—
Or shall I work the last gold stitch into my veil of state;

Or shall my woman stand and read some unimpassioned scene,—
There's music of a lulling sort in words that pause between;
Or shall she merely fan me while I wait here for the queen?

Again I caught my father's voice in sharp word of command:
'Charge!' a clash of steel: 'Charge again, the rebels stand.
Smite and spare not, hand to hand; smite and spare not, hand to
    hand.'

There swelled a tumult at the gate, high voices waxing higher;
A flash of red reflected light lit the cathedral spire;
I heard a cry for faggots, then I heard a yell for fire.

'Sit and roast there with your meat, sit and bake there with your
    bread,
You who sat to see us starve,' one shrieking woman said:
'Sit on your throne and roast with your crown upon your head.'

Nay, this thing will I do, while my mother tarrieth,
I will take my fine spun gold, but not to sew therewith,
I will take my gold and gems, and rainbow fan and wreath;

With a ransom in my lap, a king's ransom in my hand,
I will go down to this people, will stand face to face, will stand
Where they curse king, queen, and princess of this cursed land.

They shall take all to buy them bread, take all I have to give;
I, if I perish, perish; they today shall eat and live;
I, if I perish, perish – that's the goal I half conceive:

Once to speak before the world, rend bare my heart, and show
The lesson I have learned, which is death, is life, to know.
I, if I perish, perish: in the name of God I go.

Shut Out

The door was shut. I looked between
  Its iron bars; and saw it lie,
  My garden, mine, beneath the sky,
Pied with all flowers bedewed and green.

From bough to bough the song-birds crossed,
  From flower to flower the moths and bees:
  With all its nests and stately trees
It had been mine, and it was lost.

A shadowless spirit kept the gate,
  Blank and unchanging like the grave.
  I, peering through, said; 'Let me have
Some buds to cheer my outcast state.'

He answered not. 'Or give me, then,
  But one small twig from shrub or tree;
  And bid my home remember me
Until I come to it again.'

The spirit was silent; but he took
  Mortar and stone to build a wall;
  He left no loophole great or small
Through which my straining eyes might look.

So now I sit here quite alone,
  Blinded with tears; nor grieve for that,
  For nought is left worth looking at
Since my delightful land is gone.

A violet bed is budding near,
  Wherein a lark has made her nest;
  And good they are, but not the best;
And dear they are, but not so dear.

Sister Maude

Who told my mother of my shame,
   Who told my father of my dear?
Oh who but Maude, my sister Maude,
   Who lurked to spy and peer?

Cold he lies, as cold as stone,
   With his clotted curls about his face:
The comeliest corpse in all the world
   And worthy of a queen's embrace.

You might have spared his soul, sister,
   Have spared my soul, your own soul too:
Though I had not been born at all,
   He'd never have looked at you.

My father may sleep in Paradise,
   My mother at Heaven-gate:
But sister Maude shall get no sleep
   Either early or late.

My father may wear a golden gown,
   My mother a crown may win;
If my dear and I knocked at Heaven-gate
   Perhaps they'd let us in:
But sister Maude, O sister Maude,
   Bide *you* with death and sin.

Sleeping at Last

Sleeping at last, the trouble and tumult over,
   Sleeping at last, the struggle and horror past,
Cold and white, out of sight of friend and of lover,
       Sleeping at last.

No more a tired heart downcast or overcast,
No more pangs that wring or shifting fears that hover,
   Sleeping at last in a dreamless sleep locked fast.

Fast asleep. Singing birds in their leafy cover
   Cannot wake her, nor shake her the gusty blast.
Under the purple thyme and the purple clover
      Sleeping at last.

from Sonnets of Later Life

Something this foggy day, a something which
   Is neither of this fog nor of today,
   Has set me dreaming of the winds that play
Past certain cliffs, along one certain beach,
   And turn the topmost edge of waves to spray:
   Ah, pleasant pebbly strand so far away,
So out of reach while quite within my reach,
   As out of reach as India or Cathay!
I am sick of where I am and where I am not,
   I am sick of foresight and of memory,
   I am sick of all I have and all I see,
    I am sick of self, and there is nothing new;
Oh weary impatient patience of my lot!—
    Thus with myself: how fares it, Friends, with you?

Somewhere or Other

Somewhere or other there must surely be
   The face not seen, the voice not heard,
The heart that not yet – never yet – ah me!
   Made answer to my word.

Somewhere or other, may be near or far;
   Past land and sea, clean out of sight;
Beyond the wandering moon, beyond the star
   That tracks her night by night.

Somewhere or other, may be far or near;
   With just a wall, a hedge between;
With just the last leaves of the dying year
   Fallen on a turf grown green.

Song

Oh roses for the flush of youth,
   And laurel for the perfect prime;
But pluck an ivy branch for me
   Grown old before my time.

Oh violets for the grave of youth,
   And bay for those dead in their prime;
Give me the withered leaves I chose
   Before in the old time.

'Summer is Ended'

To think that this meaningless thing was ever a rose,
      Scentless, colourless, *this!*
   Will it ever be thus (who knows?)
         Thus with our bliss,
   If we wait till the close?

Though we care not to wait for the end, there comes the end
      Sooner, later, at last,

Which nothing can mar, nothing mend:
    An end locked fast,
Bent we cannot re-bend.

Symbols

I watched a rosebud very long
  Brought on by dew and sun and shower,
  Waiting to see the perfect flower:
Then, when I thought it should be strong,
  It opened at the matin hour
    And fell at evensong.

I watched a nest from day to day,
  A green nest full of pleasant shade,
  Wherein three speckled eggs were laid:
But when they should have hatched in May,
  The two old birds had grown afraid
    Or tired, and flew away.

Then in my wrath I broke the bough
  That I had tended so with care,
  Hoping its scent should fill the air;
I crushed the eggs, not heeding how
  Their ancient promise had been fair:
    I would have vengeance now.

But the dead branch spoke from the sod,
  And the eggs answered me again:
  Because we failed dost thou complain?
Is thy wrath just? And what if God,
  Who waiteth for thy fruits in vain,
    Should also take the rod?

from Sing-Song

There is one that has a head without an eye,
   And there's one that has an eye without a head:
You may find the answer if you try;
     And when all is said,
   Half the answer hangs upon a thread!

The Thread of Life

1

The irresponsive silence of the land,
   The irresponsive sounding of the sea,
   Speak both one message of one sense to me:—
'Aloof, aloof, we stand aloof; so stand
Thou too aloof bound with the flawless band
   Of inner solitude; we bind not thee;
   But who from thy self-chain shall set thee free?
What heart shall touch thy heart? what hand thy hand?'—
And I am sometimes proud and sometimes meek,
   And sometimes I remember days of old
When fellowship seemed not so far to seek
   And all the world and I seemed much less cold,
   And at the rainbow's foot lay surely gold,
And hope felt strong and life itself not weak.

2

Thus am I mine own prison. Everything
   Around me free and sunny and at ease:
   Or if in shadow, in a shade of trees
Which the sun kisses, where the gay birds sing
And where all winds make various murmuring;
   Where bees are found, with honey for the bees;
   Where sounds are music, and where silences

Are music of an unlike fashioning.
Then gaze I at the merrymaking crew,
    And smile a moment and a moment sigh,
Thinking, Why can I not rejoice with you?
    But soon I put the foolish fancy by:
I am not what I have nor what I do;
    But what I was I am, I am even I.

3

Therefore myself is that one only thing
    I hold to use or waste, to keep or give;
    My sole possession every day I live,
And still mine own despite Time's winnowing.
Ever mine own, while moons and seasons bring
    From crudeness ripeness mellow and sanative;
    Ever mine own, till Death shall ply his sieve;
And still mine own, when saints break grave and sing.
And this myself as king unto my King
    I give, to Him Who gave Himself for me;
Who gives Himself to me, and bids me sing
    A sweet new song of His redeemed set free;
He bids me sing, O Death, where is thy sting?
    And sing, O grave, where is thy victory?

The Three Enemies

THE FLESH

'Sweet, thou art pale.'
        'More pale to see,
Christ hung upon the cruel tree
And bore His Father's wrath for me.'

'Sweet, thou art sad.'
        'Beneath a rod
More heavy, Christ for my sake trod

The winepress of the wrath of God.'

'Sweet, thou art weary.'
  'Not so Christ:
Whose mighty love of me sufficed
For Strength, Salvation, Eucharist.'

'Sweet, thou art footsore.'
  'If I bleed,
His feet have bled: yea, in my need
His Heart once bled for mine indeed.'

THE WORLD

'Sweet, thou art young.'
  'So He was young
Who for my sake in silence hung
Upon the Cross with Passion wrung.'

'Look, thou art fair.'
  'He was more fair
Than men, Who deigned for me to wear
A visage marred beyond compare.'

'And thou hast riches.'
  'Daily bread:
All else is His; Who living, dead,
For me lacked where to lay His Head.'

'And life is sweet.'
  'It was not so
To Him, Whose Cup did overflow
With mine unutterable woe.'

THE DEVIL

'Thou drinkest deep.'
  'When Christ would sup
He drained the dregs from out my cup:
So how should I be lifted up?'

'Thou shalt win Glory.'
    'In the skies,
Lord Jesus, cover up mine eyes
Lest they should look on vanities.'

'Thou shalt have Knowledge.'
    'Helpless dust,
In Thee, O Lord, I put my trust:
Answer Thou for me, Wise and Just.'

'And Might.'—
    'Get thee behind me. Lord,
Who hast redeemed and not abhorred
My soul, oh keep it by Thy Word.'

from Three Stages

A Pause of Thought

I looked for that which is not, nor can be,
    And hope deferred made my heart sick in truth:
    But years must pass before a hope of youth
      Is resigned utterly.

I watched and waited with a steadfast will:
    And though the object seemed to flee away
    That I so longed for, ever day by day
      I watched and waited still.

Sometimes I said: 'This thing shall be no more;
    My expectation wearies and shall cease;
    I will resign it now and be at peace':
      Yet never gave it o'er.

Sometimes I said: 'It is an empty name
    I long for; to a name why should I give

The peace of all the days I have to live?'—
    Yet gave it all the same.

Alas thou foolish one! alike unfit
    For healthy joy and salutary pain:
    Thou knowest the chase useless, and again
        Turnest to follow it.

To Lalla, reading my verses topsy-turvy

Darling little Cousin,
    With your thoughtful look
Reading topsy-turvy
    From a printed book

English hieroglyphics,
    More mysterious
To you, than Egyptian
    Ones would be to us;—

Leave off for a minute
    Studying, and say
What is the impression
    That those marks convey?

Only solemn silence,
    And a wondering smile:
But your eyes are lifted
    Unto mine the while.

In their gaze so steady
    I can surely trace
That a happy spirit
    Lighteth up your face.

Tender, happy spirit,
   Innocent and pure;
Teaching more than science,
   And than learning more.

How should I give answer
   To that asking look?
Darling little Cousin
   Go back to your book.

Read on: if you knew it,
   You have cause to boast:—
You are much the wisest,
   Though I know the most.

A Triad

Three sang of love together: one with lips
   Crimson, with cheeks and bosom in a glow,
Flushed to the yellow hair and finger tips;
   And one there sang who soft and smooth as snow
   Bloomed like a tinted hyacinth at a show;
And one was blue with famine after love,
   Who like a harpstring snapped rang harsh and low
The burden of what those were singing of.
One shamed herself in love; one temperately
   Grew gross in soulless love, a sluggish wife;
One famished died for love. Thus two of three
   Took death for love and won him after strife;
One droned in sweetness like a fattened bee:
   All on the threshold, yet all short of life.

Twice

I took my heart in my hand,
   (O my love, O my love),
I said: Let me fall or stand,
   Let me live or die,
But this once hear me speak—
   (O my love, O my love)—
Yet a woman's words are weak;
   You should speak, not I.

You took my heart in your hand
   With a friendly smile,
With a critical eye you scanned,
   Then set it down,
And said: It is still unripe,
   Better wait awhile;
Wait while the skylarks pipe,
   Till the corn grows brown.

As you set it down it broke—
   Broke, but I did not wince;
I smiled at the speech you spoke,
   At your judgment that I heard:
But I have not often smiled
   Since then, nor questioned since,
Nor cared for corn-flowers wild,
   Nor sung with the singing bird.

I take my heart in my hand,
   O my God, O my God,
My broken heart in my hand:
   Thou hast seen, judge Thou.
My hope was written on sand,
   O my God, O my God:
Now let Thy judgment stand—
   Yea, judge me now.

This contemned of a man,
   This marred one heedless day,

This heart take Thou to scan
　　Both within and without:
Refine with fire its gold,
　　Purge Thou its dross away—
Yea hold it in Thy hold,
　　Whence none can pluck it out.

I take my heart in my hand—
　　I shall not die, but live—
Before Thy face I stand;
　　I, for Thou callest such:
All that I have I bring,
　　All that I am I give;
Smile Thou and I shall sing,
　　But shall not question much.

from Sing-Song

Twist me a crown of wind-flowers;
　　That I may fly away
To hear the singers at their song,
　　And players at their play.

Put on your crown of wind-flowers:
　　But whither would you go?
Beyond the surging of the sea
　　And the storms that blow.

Alas! your crown of wind-flowers
　　Can never make you fly:
　　I twist them in a crown today,
　　　　And tonight they die.

*

Under the ivy bush
  One sits sighing,
And under the willow tree
  One sits crying:—

Under the ivy bush
  Cease from your sighing,
But under the willow tree
  Lie down a-dying.

Up-Hill

'Does the road wind up-hill all the way?'
  'Yes, to the very end.'
'Will the day's journey take the whole long day?'
  'From morn to night, my friend.'

'But is there for the night a resting-place?'
  'A roof for when the slow dark hours begin.'
'May not the darkness hide it from my face?'
  'You cannot miss that inn.'

'Shall I meet other wayfarers at night?'
  'Those who have gone before.'
'Then must I knock, or call when just in sight?'
  'They will not keep you standing at that door.'

'Shall I find comfort, travel-sore and weak?'
  'Of labour you shall find the sum.'
'Will there be beds for me and all who seek?'
  'Yea, beds for all who come.'

Weary in Well-Doing

I would have gone; God bade me stay:
   I would have worked; God bade me rest.
He broke my will from day to day;
   He read my yearnings unexprest,
     And said them nay.

Now I would stay; God bids me go;
   Now I would rest; God bids me work.
He breaks my heart tost to and fro;
   My soul is wrung with doubts that lurk
     And vex it so.

I go, Lord, where Thou sendest me;
   Day after day I plod and moil:
But, Christ my God, when will it be
   That I may let alone my toil
     And rest with Thee?

from Sing-Song

What are heavy? sea-sand and sorrow:
What are brief? today and tomorrow:
What are frail? Spring blossoms and youth:
What are deep? the ocean and truth.

       *

What does the bee do?
   Bring home honey.
And what does Father do?
   Bring home money.
And what does Mother do?

Lay out the money.
And what does baby do?
Eat up the honey.

Song

When I am dead, my dearest,
   Sing no sad songs for me;
Plant thou no roses at my head,
   Nor shady cypress tree:
Be the green grass above me
   With showers and dewdrops wet:
And if thou wilt, remember,
   And if thou wilt, forget.

I shall not see the shadows,
   I shall not feel the rain;
I shall not hear the nightingale
   Sing on as if in pain:
And dreaming through the twilight
   That doth not rise nor set,
Haply I may remember,
   And haply may forget.

Where shall I find a white rose?

Where shall I find a white rose blowing?—
   Out in the garden where all sweets be.—
But out in my garden the snow was snowing
   And never a white rose opened for me.
Nought but snow and a wind were blowing
   And snowing.

Where shall I find a blush rose blushing?—
  On the garden wall or the garden bed.—
But out in my garden the rain was rushing
  And never a blush rose raised its head.
Nothing glowing, flushing or blushing:
      Rain rushing.

Where shall I find a red rose budding?—
  Out in the garden where all things grow.—
But out in my garden a flood was flooding
  And never a red rose began to blow.
Out in a flooding what should be budding?
      All flooding!

Now is winter and now is sorrow,
  No roses but only thorns today:
Thorns will put on roses tomorrow,
  Winter and sorrow scudding away.
No more winter and no more sorrow
      Tomorrow.

from Sing-Song

Who has seen the wind?
  Neither I nor you:
But when the leaves hang trembling
  The wind is passing through.

Who has seen the wind?
  Neither you nor I:
But when the trees bow down their heads
  The wind is passing by.

Who Shall Deliver Me?

God strengthen me to bear myself;
That heaviest weight of all to bear,
Inalienable weight of care.

All others are outside myself;
I lock my door and bar them out,
The turmoil, tedium, gad-about.

I lock my door upon myself,
And bar them out; but who shall wall
Self from myself, most loathed of all?

If I could once lay down myself,
And start self-purged upon the race
That all must run! Death runs apace.

If I could set aside myself,
And start with lightened heart upon
The road by all men overgone!

God harden me against myself,
This coward with pathetic voice
Who craves for ease, and rest, and joys:

Myself, arch-traitor to myself;
My hollowest friend, my deadliest foe,
My clog whatever road I go.

Yet One there is can curb myself,
Can roll the strangling load from me,
Break off the yoke and set me free.

Winter: My Secret

I tell my secret? No indeed, not I:
Perhaps some day, who knows?
But not today; it froze, and blows, and snows,
And you're too curious: fie!
You want to hear it? well:
Only, my secret's mine, and I won't tell.

Or, after all, perhaps there's none:
Suppose there is no secret after all,
But only just my fun.
Today's a nipping day, a biting day;
In which one wants a shawl,
A veil, a cloak, and other wraps:
I cannot ope to every one who taps,
And let the draughts come whistling through my hall;
Come bounding and surrounding me,
Come buffeting, astounding me,
Nipping and clipping through my wraps and all.
I wear my mask for warmth: who ever shows
His nose to Russian snows
To be pecked at by every wind that blows?
You would not peck? I thank you for good will,
Believe, but leave that truth untested still.

Spring's an expansive time: yet I don't trust
March with its peck of dust,
Nor April with its rainbow-crowned brief showers,
Nor even May, whose flowers
One frost may wither through the sunless hours.

Perhaps some languid summer day,
When drowsy birds sing less and less,
And golden fruit is ripening to excess,
If there's not too much sun nor too much cloud,
And the warm wind is neither still nor loud,
Perhaps my secret I may say,
Or you may guess.

A Wish

I wish I were a little bird
    That out of sight doth soar;
I wish I were a song once heard
    But often pondered o'er,
Or shadow of a lily stirred
    By wind upon the floor,
Or echo of a loving word
    Worth all that went before,
Or memory of a hope deferred
    That springs again no more.

The World

By day she woos me, soft, exceeding fair:
    But all night as the moon so changeth she;
    Loathsome and foul with hideous leprosy,
And subtle serpents gliding in her hair.
By day she woos me to the outer air,
    Ripe fruits, sweet flowers, and full satiety:
    But through the night a beast she grins at me,
A very monster void of love and prayer.
By day she stands a lie: by night she stands
    In all the naked horror of the truth,
With pushing horns and clawed and clutching hands.
Is this a friend indeed, that I should sell
    My soul to her, give her my life and youth,
Till my feet, cloven too, take hold on hell?

Notes

'Behold, I stand at the door': title from Revelation 3:20. The speaker in the final stanza is Jesus Christ.

Bird or Beast?: in Christian theology, dove and lamb are symbolic of Christ.

A Birthday: line 10 vair: fur, represented in heraldry as blue and silver.

A Coast: Nightmare: sometimes known simply as 'A Nightmare'.

The Convent Threshold: inspired by the story of Abelard and Heloise.

Despised and Rejected: line 8 'Friend, open to Me': the speaker is Christ.

A Dumb Friend: line 28 cypress trees: symbolic of graveyards.

Jessie Cameron: line 53 grandam: grandmother; **line 59: unked:** dismal (dialect)

Kookoorookoo! both this and 'kikirikee' are onomatopoeic renderings of the sound of cocks crowing.

L. E. L.: initials under which poet Letitia Elizabeth Landon (1802–38) wrote; **line 36   scathe:** injury, punishment.

O Lord, when Thou didst call me: dialogue between Christ and the soul.

Monna Innominata: the title means 'unknown' or anonymous lady. A 'sonnet of sonnets' is a sequence of fourteen sonnets corresponding to the fourteen lines in a sonnet.

Beatrice: beloved by the famous Italian poet Dante. **Laura**: beloved by the next famous Italian poet Petrarch. **donne innominate**: nameless or unknown ladies. **less conspicuous poets:** troubadours. **that land:** Provence in the thirteenth century. **Great Poetess:** Elizabeth Barrett Browning, author of 'Sonnets from the Portuguese' celebrating love fulfilled. **Epigraphs:** (translations by William Michael Rossetti) **1** 'The day that they have said adieu to their sweet friends.' 'Love, with how great a stress dost thou vanquish me today!' **2** 'It was already the hour which turns back the desire.' 'I recur to the time when I first saw thee.' **3** 'Oh shades, empty save in semblances.' 'An imaginary guide conducts her.' **4** 'A small spark fosters a great flame.' 'Every other thing, every other thought, goes off, and love alone remains there with you.' **5** 'Love, who exempts no loved one from loving.' 'Love led me into such joyous hope.' **6** 'Now canst thou comprehend the quantity of the love which glows in me towards thee.' 'I do not choose that Love should release me from such a lie.' **7** 'Here always Spring and every fruit.' 'Conversing with me, and I with him.' **8** 'As if he were to say to God, "I care for nought else".' 'I hope to find pity and not only pardon.' **9** 'O dignified and pure conscience!' 'Spirit more lit with burning virtues.' **10** 'With better course and not with better star.' 'Life flees, and stays not an hour.' **11** 'Come after me, and leave folk to talk.' 'Relating the casualties of our life.' **12** 'Love, who speaks within my mind.' 'Love comes in the beautiful face of this woman.' **13** 'And we will direct our eyes to the primal Love.' 'But I find a burden to which my arms suffice not.' **14** 'And His will is our peace.' 'Only with these thoughts, with different locks.' *Sonnet 8:* **line 1 Esther:** biblical heroine who saved the Jewish people. *Sonnet 11:* **line 5 prate:** gossip, chatter.

The Queen of Hearts: **line 13 prepense:** intentionally.

Roses on a Brier: alternate spelling of 'briar'.

A Royal Princess: **line 93 faggots:** firewood.

There is one that has a head: a pin and a needle, of course!

The Three Enemies: three dialogues between the soul and (a) the body or flesh; (b) worldly desires; (c) the devil.

The World: in Victorian theology, 'the world' of material pleasure and self-indulgence signified evil, in contrast to spiritual or heavenly aspiration. **line 6 satiety:** satisfaction, fullness.

Index of First Lines